SCOTLAND'S SPORTING CURIOSITIES

SCOTLAND'S SPORTING
CURIOSITIES

Jim Craig

BIRLINN

First published in 2005 by Birlinn Ltd
West Newington House
10 Newington Road
Edinburgh EH9 1QS

www.birlinn.co.uk

ISBN10: 1 84158 336 7
ISBN: 978 1 84158 336 5

British Library Cataloguing-in-Publication Data
A catalogue record for this book is available from
the British Library

Typesetting by IMH(Cartrif), Loanhead, Scotland
Printed and bound by Creative Print and Design, Wales

CONTENTS

Author's Note	vi
Introduction	vii
Athletics	1
Bowling	17
Boxing	21
Climbing	35
Cricket	39
Football	51
Gold Medallists	121
Golf	133
Hockey	147
Motor sports	155
Olympics	161
Rugby	169
Sailing	201
Snooker	205
Swimming	211
Various sports	217

Angling	219
Ball games	219
Chess	221
Croquet	221
Curling	222
Cycling	223
Darts	226
Dog racing	227
Horse racing	228
Ice hockey	229
Judo	230
Rowing	231
Shinty	231
Table Tennis	233
Tennis	234
Walking	235
General	235

Scottish Sports Hall of Fame	239

AUTHOR'S NOTE

Perhaps a little clarification of the title might be useful at this point and for that, two definitions from my trusty dictionary are necessary.

The first is 'curious' – odd or unusual; and the second is 'curiosities' – rare or curious objects.

Now, in the course of the following 250 or so pages, the reader will certainly find the odd, the unusual and even the bizarre occurrences covering a wide range of sports. However, it may surprise some people that I have also included many examples when Scots have risen to the challenge and performed well in their respective fields.

Unfortunately, for a number of reasons – like uncertain weather, the size of the population, poor training facilities and lack of regard for the benefits of sport – Scottish successes at top level can be infrequent or indeed, rare. Hence the title, *Scotland's Sporting Curiosities*.

INTRODUCTION

Early forms of sporting endeavour, from around 7th century BC to late 11th century AD

The history of Scotland is quite a complicated tale. Through the centuries, various tribes and peoples invaded the land, some for short, often violent visits, others to find a new home.

The original inhabitants were supposed to have been of Iberian stock and around 7th century BC they began to mingle with the invading Celts. The latter had originated in south-west Germany but later spread through France, northern Spain and the British Isles.

Meanwhile, the Scots, a Celtic tribe from Ireland, had settled in the west of the country; the Picts, a fairly warlike tribe, had occupied the north; while invaders from Germany took over many parts of the east coast.

No doubt the men and women of these peoples spent most of their days occupied with the necessities of life. Meat had to be hunted or reared, fish caught, fields tilled and crops cared for; clothes and some form of shoes had to be fashioned; basic housing put up; water gathered. The women would spend a good part of the day preparing food; the men practised for war, in areas like archery, sword-play or the use of the pike.

Certainly, a busy life, yet I cannot believe that at some points of it a more light-hearted side did not come in. I would be astonished if there were not foot-races, for instance, or a throwing competition, or even a form of ball-game, the 'ball' consisting of rags tied together.

Just consider the various sports and/or athletic events which might have been employed – in whatever embryonic form – in everyday life. A river or stream to be crossed? Well, you could row or sail some primitive craft or even swim.

A distance to be covered? You could walk, run, or even ride! A heavy stone blocking one's path? A spot of weightlifting will soon clear that. Smaller stones or lighter objects needing to be moved some distance?

Why not throw them, move them along the ground by hitting them with a stick (hockey or golf) or even strike them in the air with a club (tennis or baseball).

Certainly, by the time of the Romans – from 55 BC onwards – sport and leisure were features of their everyday life. Julius Caesar had not simply brought some dedicated troops to our land; he brought harpastum, a game which could be described as follows: 'The players divide themselves into two bands. The ball is thrown upon the line in the middle. At the two ends behind the places where the players are stationed there are two other lines, beyond which they tried to carry the ball, a feat that could not be done without pushing one another backward and forward.' Does that not sound like a basic form of rugby? Or even a fairly primitive form of football, before proper rules were brought in?

Unfortunately, there are few, if any, written records from those early days. For the first definitive report of a sporting contest, we have to come forward to the late 11th century, when Malcolm Ceann-Mor was King of Scotland. He wanted to organise a collection of fast runners to carry messages throughout the Highlands and Lowlands of his kingdom, so he issued an edict for the clans to gather at the Braes of Mar.

In order to select the quickest among those gathered, the King organised a race to the summit of Creag Choinnich overlooking Braemar. Was this the first hill race ever held in Scotland?

ATHLETICS

A Scot takes the top sprint: Alan Wells

The unofficial title of the 'Fastest Man in the World' is usually awarded to the winner of the 100 metres at the Olympic Games. Traditionally, these winners come from sunny climes in countries where good training facilities are taken for granted. For many years, the vast majority were Americans.

In fact, since the Modern Olympics began in 1896, only Reg Walker (South Africa – 1908), Harold Abrahams (GB – 1924), Percy Williams (Canada – 1928), Armin Hary (West Germany – 1960) and Valeri Borzov (USSR – 1976) had broken the US domination before Alan Wells stepped up for the 1980 final in Moscow.

Alan Wipper Wells was a late developer in athletics, only just breaking 11 seconds for the 100 metres at the age of 24 in 1976. Two years later, though, he equalled Peter Radford's 20–year-old UK record of 10.29, and six days after that, brought it down to 10.15 secs. One month on again, in August 1978, at the Commonwealth Games in Edmonton, Wells took silver in the 100 metres, gold in the 200 metres and also anchored the Scottish 4 x 100 metres squad to victory.

In 1979, Alan Wells twice improved the UK 200 metres record and took the scalp of Italian world record-holder Pietro Mennea in the European Cup final. All these times by Wells had been achieved without the use of starting blocks, but due to a change in IAAF regulations, these became compulsory for the Moscow Olympics.

Wells soon showed that he had mastered them when he set a UK record of 10.11 seconds in the heats of the 100 metres and he ran equally well in his semi-final.

At 5 p.m. in the Lenin Stadium, on a sultry July evening, Wells went to his work in the outside lane, number eight, with his chief rival Silvio Leonard of Cuba in number one. As the gun went off, both men blasted into action. To begin with, all eight finalists looked in contention. By halfway, though, Wells and Leonard were pulling away from the rest, competing nip and tuck all the way to the tape. As both dipped towards it, Wells just had the edge, becoming the first Scot to become 'the fastest man in the world'.

The time of 10.25 seconds was not the quickest but Wells not only became the oldest winner up to that time, he showed that a sprint champion could come from a country with inclement weather and poor training facilities.

Athletic Scots

Several Scottish athletes have won titles in major international championships outwith the Olympics and the Commonwealth Games:

World Athletic Championships

10,000 metres	Liz McColgan	1991

World Road Race Championships

Women's Half Marathon	Liz McColgan	1992

IAAF World Indoor Championships

800 metres	Tom McKean	1993
3000 metres	Yvonne Murray	1993

European Championships

200 metres	Dougie Walker	1998
400 metres	David Jenkins	1971
800 metres	Tom McKean	1990
5000 metres	Ian Stewart	1969
High Jump	Alan Paterson	1950
4 x 100 metres relay	Dougie Walker*	1992
4 x 400 metres relay	Angus Scott*	1950
	John McIsaac*	1958
	David Jenkins*	1974
	Brian Whittle*	1986
3000 metres	Yvonne Murray	1990
4 x 400 metres relay	Rosemary Stirling*	1969

*Part of GB squad

European Indoor Championships

800 metres	Tom McKean	1990
3000 metres	Ian Stewart	1969 & 1975
	Peter Stewart	1971
3000 metres	Yvonne Murray	1987

Athletic shorts

At Celtic Park, Glasgow, on 20 July 1895, a Scotland team took part in its first athletic international when Ireland were the visitors.

This was the first of an unbroken series (1895 to 1913), of which Ireland won 11, Scotland 7, with 1 contest halved.

————

Football grounds have hosted international athletic matches on a number of occasions:

Scotland v Ireland	1895	Celtic Park
Scotland v Ireland	1907, 1910	Ibrox Park
Scotland v Ireland & England	1914, 1922, 1930	Hampden Park

Football grounds have also hosted the Scottish Amateur Athletic Championships:

Celtic Park	1897, 1913, 1919, 1921, 1923
Ibrox Park	1895, 1903, 1905, 1909, 1912
Hampden Park	1897, 1913, 1919, 1921, 1923, 1924, 1927, 1929–39 and 1945–51

————

Between 1903 and 1923, Tom Nicholson won the SAAA shot putt title 14 times. His younger brother Andrew then went on to win the event 11 times. Tom Nicholson also won the Hammer Throw title 21 times between between 1902 and 1927.

————

For five consecutive seasons – 1921 to 1925 – Eric Liddell won both the 100 yards and 200 yards titles at the Scottish Amateur Athletics Championships. In 1924 and 1925 Liddell also won the 440 yards title.

Crawford W. Fairbrother won the SAAA High Jump title between 1957 and 1969 (13 times).

A very determined lady

As Liz Lynch from Dundee, Liz McColgan's interest in athletics began at a very early age.

Lynch studied at the University of Alabama and then returned to Scotland to pursue her running career, winning the gold medal in the 10,000 metres at the Commonwealth Games at Edinburgh in 1986.

After her marriage to another athlete, Peter McColgan, she won the silver medal at the same distance in the 1988 Olympics and in the 1990 Commonwealth Games, Liz McColgan retained her 10,000 metres title as well as taking bronze in the 3,000 metres.

Only months after giving birth to her first child, McColgan won the 10,000-metres event in the World Athletic Championships at Tokyo in 1990. She now runs a health club with her husband and is the chairperson of scottishathletics.

A strong legend in his own lifetime: Donald Dinnie

Born in 1837, at Balnacriag, near Aboyne, Donald Dinnie became a legend of the 19th-century Highland Games circuit. A stonemason by trade, he became a professional athlete in his late twenties and won his last prize at the age of 76! During his career, Dinnie toured Australia, America and South Africa, won around 11,000 prizes and £26,000 in prize money.

Unfortunately, many of his medals are now missing, perhaps having been sold when he fell on hard times towards the end of his life. Some are held in a collection by Aberdeen Art Gallery and Museums, the earliest dated 1859 for 'heavy' events at Glenisla and Perth, and the latest dated 1884 for Club Swimming in Brisbane, Australia.

The four big events for the 'heavies' are Stone Putting, Weight Throwing (56 lb), Hammer Throwing and Caber Tossing. In the hammer throw, Dinnie developed a 'round the head' technique in the

1850s, a style adopted by many of his counterparts and still used today.

Dinnie's most successful event was the caber toss, in which he won 1400 contests and was unbeaten for 40 years! Outside of the Highland Games, Dinnie was also an excellent weightlifter. And it was in the field of weightlifting that his memory best lives on. In his teenage years, while helping his father to repair the Potarch Bridge, over the River Dee, near Kincardine O'Neil, Dinnie showed colossal strength as he carried two huge boulders totalling 785 lb in weight across the bridge. The 'Dinnie Steens' are now legendary and nobody has ever matched this amazing feat without using a harness.

First four-minute miler from Scotland

As soon as Roger Bannister went through the 4-minute barrier, in 1954, many others were keen to follow in his footsteps.

In Scotland, Alan Gordon and Graham Everett were among the names to the fore, while down south, Anglo-Scots like Mike Beresford rose to the challenge. Their times, however, were still some distance off the magical figure.

Indeed, when Derek Ibbotson ran the first-ever 4-minute mile in Scotland – at the Glasgow Police Sports in 1957 – his 3 mins 58.4 secs win was followed by Beresford's second place time of 4 mins 6 secs, with Everett in third place in 4 mins 6.6 secs.

By 1958, Everett had improved to 4 mins 3.5; a month earlier, Beresford had recorded the same time in the Great Britain versus Commonwealth match. In 1960, Everett went lower again, 4 mins 2.8 secs in the AAA Championships at the White City but although he carried on competing until 1964, this proved to be his best time at the event. Beresford continued to bring his time down. On 4 May 1961 he clocked 4 mins 2.1 secs; nine days later he lowered it again to 4 mins 1.4. Then, on 18 August of that year, in the Emsley Carr Mile at the White City, he was finally drawn to the sub-4-minute regions. The race was won by Jim Beatty of the USA (3 mins 56.5) and although Mike Beresford finished a distant 5th in the race, he became the first Scot to dip under the 4-minute barrier when he recorded 3 mins 59.2. Another eight years would pass before another Scot bettered the 4-minute time.

The town of Reading in Berkshire seems an unlikely spot for a landmark in Scottish miling history, even more so when the meeting was the Reading Chronicle's 'Gala Night of Sport'.

In the mile race that night – 11 June 1969 – were 3 Scots, Ian McCafferty from Law and the Stewart brothers, Ian and Peter, whose father had moved from Musselburgh to Birmingham some 20 years before. By prior arrangement, a pacemaker led through the first lap, passing the quarter-mile in 58.1secs.

At the halfway point (1 min 58.9), the 25–year-old McCafferty took over, only to be overtaken at the midway point of the third lap by Ian Stewart, who took them through the bell. With 220 yards to go, McCafferty broke to the front, and although challenged strongly by the Stewarts, maintained his form to win by 3 yards in 3 mins 56.8 secs, his first-ever mile under 4 minutes. Behind him, Ian (3 mins 57.3) and Peter (3 mins 58.7) also created personal bests, becoming the first Scots brothers to break the 4-minute barrier. McCafferty also became the first home Scot to do so.

A year later, again in the Emsley Carr Mile, although this time at Meadowbank Stadium in Edinburgh, the Stewart brothers treated the near capacity crowd to a wonderful display of miling. They were both timed at 3 mins 57.4 secs, although Ian got the verdict by the thickness of a vest. It was the first 4-minute mile in Scotland since Derek Ibbotson's effort thirteen years before.

First SAAA championships: 1880s

The Scottish Amateur Athletic Association was founded on 26 February 1883 and wasted no time in organizing an inaugural national championship meeting, which took place at Powderhall Grounds, Edinburgh on Saturday, 23 June 1883.

In bright, sunny weather 3000 turned out to watch the proceedings; for the winners, there would be a silver medal, with a bronze for the runners-up. 30 competitors took part, all of whom had to adhere to the SAAA's definition of 'amateur': 'An amateur is one who has never competed for a money prize, or a staked belt, or with or against a professional for any prize, or who has never taught, pursued or assisted in the practice of athletic exercises as a means of obtaining a livelihood.'

From the wing to an Olympic gold: Eric Liddell, 1920s

In 1922 and 1923 Eric Liddell played seven times on the wing for Scotland at rugby. He only finished on the losing side once, in the 1923 Calcutta Cup match against England at Inverleith, but he scored tries against Wales, France and Ireland before giving up the game to concentrate on athletics.

This story, or rather a fictional account of it, was the subject of the film *Chariots of Fire*. In truth, the reality was even stranger. Liddell was a natural sprinter, his time of 9.7 seconds for the 100 yards in 1923 standing as a British record for 35 years.

When the programme of events was announced for the Paris Olympics of 1924, Liddell immediately abandoned any idea of running in the 100 metres as the heats would be held on a Sunday, quite anathema to his religious principles. Instead, he decided to compete in the 200 and 400 metres.

When he walked in to the Colombes Stadium for the heats of the 200 metres, Liddell must have felt some familiarity with his surroundings as he had made his international rugby debut there two years before. Perhaps this setting inspired him, because he raised his level of performance, firstly to take the bronze medal in the 200 metres and then, in a classic final in the 400 metres, he somehow managed to maintain his devastating early pace all the way to the tape, coming home in 47.6 seconds for a new British, European and Olympic record.

After winning three events in the 1925 Scottish Championships, Liddell returned to China, the land of his birth, to join in the work of his father, a missionary. He did not give up athletics completely. In 1929, he ran 49.1 to beat the celebrated German runner Otto Peltzer and he

9

won the North China Championship. There were also reports of him playing the occasional rugby match with army staff.

Over the years which followed, Liddell devoted all his energies to his work with the church, becoming a legend in the London Missionary Society. In March 1943 he was interned in a Japanese concentration camp, where the conditions took their toll of even the fittest and strongest. Eric Liddell died at Weihsien on 21 February 1945.

It started in Hamilton: cross-country racing, 1903

The International Cross-Country Championships were first held at Hamilton Park Racecourse on 28 March 1903. A race over 8 miles (12.87 km) was contested only by the four home nations but, with the event being held annually, other European nations came in at different times, like France in 1907 and Belgium in 1923.

The first non-European entrant was Tunisia in 1958; the first Oceanic team was New Zealand in 1965; and the USA took part for the first time in 1966.

A junior race was first added in 1961 and the first women's event took place at Barry, Wales, in 1967.

Three Scots have won the men's title. James Wilson in 1930, James Flockhart in 1937 and Ian Stewart in 1970. Jim Brown won the junior men's race in 1973.

Milers: Scots under four minutes, 1960s–90s

To date, nineteen Scots athletes have run the one mile in under four minutes. These are listed below, along with their best times:

Time	Name	Position	Place	Date
3:50:64	Graeme Williamson	4	Cork	13/7/82
3:52:44	John Robson	8	Oslo	11/7/81
3:54:20	Frank Clement	4	Oslo	27/6/78
3:54:30	David Strang	9	Oslo	22/7/94
3:55:30	Peter Stewart	1	London	10/6/72
3:56:80	Ian McCafferty	1	Reading	11/6/69
3:56:90	Ron Speirs	4	Philadelphia	30/4/77
3:57:40	Ian Stewart	1	Edinburgh	13/6/70

Time	Name	Position	Place	Date
3:57:59	Adrian Weatherhead	7	London	29/8/75
3:57:60	Ian Gillespie	1	Exeter	16/6/98
3:58:05	Dave McMeekin	6	London	30/8/76
3:58:28	Adrian Callan	3	Swansea	13/7/86
3:58:70	Norman Morrison	4	Leicester	31/5/71
3:58:80	Lawrie Spence	4	Gateshead	12/9/77
3:59:10	Ron MacDonald	1	Gateshead	1/9/75
3:59:24	Mike Beresford	5	London	18/8/62
3:59:29	Alistair Currie	7	London	2/8/85
3:59:56	Glen Stewart	10	Sheffield	25/8/96
3:59:58	Colin Hulme	1	Murfreesboro	5/3/83

New Year sprint 1870s–1990s

A handicap race held over a variable distance, the New Year Sprint has been staged in Scotland on or around New Year's Day annually since 1870.

For many years known as the 'Powderhall' because of its first and most regular venue, the event started in the heyday of pedestrianism (professional footracing), the sport of the people before football. The format has not changed over the years. All races are handicapped to ensure close finishes and spectators can lay bets on the outcome. For the athletes themselves, this is the 'Big Sprint' and they train all year round with this day in mind.

Early days

As the race was always a handicap sprint, the quickest runner in the field did not always win. The name of Harry Hutchens is missing from the list of winners, but he was the fastest sprinter of the last two decades of the 19th century, having the handicap of starting at 'scratch' from 1880 to 1895. The record run of this period was by Alf Downer of Edinburgh in 1898; he ran 128.5 yards in 12.4 seconds. Tribute must also be paid to D. Wight of Jedburgh, winner of the inaugural race in 1870 off 12 yards; seven years later he repeated the win, this time off scratch.

The event continued throughout the First World War, when the great Australian champion Jack Donaldson and England's Willie Applegarth showed their class, although the prize went elsewhere.

And probably the most famous winner of all was Willie McFaralane of Glasgow, who achieved the unique distinction of winning the race two years in succession, the second time from scratch, in 1934, a feat never repeated.

Post-war years

During the late 1940s, Albert Spence was a top name in the event. He ran in five finals and won in 1947. Australian star Eric Cumming took the sprint in 1952; but Barnie Ewall of the USA, second in the 100 metres at the 1948 Olympiad, missed out. In the 1960s and '70s, while many top-class names competed in the event, two stood out: Ricky Dunbar of Edinburgh, who won in 1963 and George McNeill from Tranent, winner in 1970 and still the world record-holder for the 120 yards.

Recent years

In the 1980s two Americans from San Diego stamped their authority on the sprint. 'Kipper' Bell from San Diego was the victor in 1984 and Bill Snoddy in 1987; but for the USA boycott of the 1980 Olympics, Snoddy would have been in Moscow. And the 1980s also saw several reinstated former winners return to the amateur scene and perform well – Roy Heron (1978), Gus McQuaig (1981), Andrew Walker (1982), Neil Turnbull (1983), and Willie Fraser (1985).

The 124th Sprint in 1993 saw amateur runners competing alongside professionals for the first time as the result of an agreement between the Scottish Games' Association and the British Amateur Athletic Association.

So near, yet so far: Alistair McCorquodale, 1948

Just after the Second World War, an Anglo-Scottish sprinter shot to prominence and nearly pulled off one of the biggest prizes in the sport.

Alistair McCorquodale, born in Glasgow in December 1925, was a lieutenant in the Coldstream Guards, a barrel-chested determined competitor in athletics, rugby and cricket, at all of which he attained the highest class.

He first came to prominence in athletics when he finished fifth in the 1947 AAA 100 yards final. One year later, he had improved to second and also took the 220 yards title in 22.2 seconds; a fortnight on again, he won the 100 metres at the triangular home international encounter at Manchester in 10.8 seconds.

As he headed for the London Olympics shortly afterwards, McCorquodale's times could not realistically be compared with Americans like Mel Patton, Barney Ewell, or Harrison Dillard. Like any good competitor, though, McCorquodale rose to the occasion, making an improvement of around three metres or so for times of 10.5 seconds in both first and second rounds, and 10.7 seconds in the semi-finals.

In the final were the three Americans plus Lloyd La Beach from Panama and British champion, McDonald Bailey. From the gun, the powerful London Scottish forward matched strides all the way with these great runners and at the finish was placed fourth, a mere one-tenth of a second behind the winner, Harrison Dillard.

It was a fabulous performance by McCorquodale in his first season, and a few days later, he picked up a silver medal as part of the GB 4 x 100 metres relay team.

Shortly afterwards, at Hampden Park, in June 1948, Alistair McCorquodale set a new Scottish native 120 yards record of 11.6 seconds. He then faded out of athletics to join the family printing firm and his achievements were soon overlooked. Yet surely any sprinter who was only one-tenth of a second away from gold deserves to be remembered.

The long–distance Scot: Don Ritchie, 1970s–90s

Born in July 1944 at Haddowhouse in Aberdeenshire, Don Ritchie started competitive running in his teenage years but only gravitated towards the ultra distances from 1970 onwards. Since then, Ritchie has had a remarkable career.

In fact, Don Ritchie has so many World Bests, Veteran World Bests, Championship Titles and other astonishing performances to his credit that we simply do not have the space in this book to give a definitive listing. The details below will give some idea of his range and ability:

Absolute world best performances (world records)

Event	Time	Date	Location
50 km	2 hr 51m 38s	29.04.77	Epsom
150 km*	10 hr 3m 47s	25.09.77	Crystal Palace
100 miles*	11 hr 30m 51s	25.09.77	Crystal Palace
100 km	6 hr 18m 00s	30.06.78	Hartola, Finland
50 miles	4 hr 53m 28s	28.10.78	Crystal Palace
100 km*	6 hr 10m 20s	28.10.78	Crystal Palace
50 km	2 hr 50m 30s	10.03.79	Altrincham
100 miles (road)	11 hr 51m 11s	16.06.79	New York
40 miles	3 hr 48m 35s	16.10.82	Copthall
50 miles	4 hr 51m 49s	12.03.83	Copthall
200 km	16 hr 32m 30s	30.10.83	Coatbridge
200 km (indoors)	16 hr 31m 08s	04.02.90	Milton Keynes
24 hrs (indoors)	166 miles 429 yards	03.02.90	Milton Keynes
200 km*	16 hr 19m 16s	26.10.91	Copthall

* These records are currently held.

World veteran best performances

Event	Time	Date	Location
Over 40			
100 km	6hr 36m 02s	04.05.86	Turin to St Vincent
Over 45			
40 miles*	4 hr 15m 15s	24.06.90	Livingston
50 miles*	5 hr 23m 02s	24.06.90	Livingston
100 km	6 hr 46m 10s	24.06.90	Livingston
100 km	6 hr 40m 23s	06.10.90	Santander, Spain
100 miles*	12 hr 44m 28s	26.10.91	Copthall
200 km*	16 hr 19m 16s	26.10.91	Copthall
24 hrs*	166 miles 1203 yds	26.10.91	Copthall

Event	Time	Date	Location
Over 50			
30 miles*	3 hr 10m 15s	05.03.95	Barry
50 km*	3 hr 17m 21s	05.03.95	Barry
40 miles*	4 hr 21m 34s	05.03.95	Barry
50 miles*	5 hr 37m 17s	14.10.95	Tooting
100 kms*	7 hr 07m 29s	14.10.95	Tooting

*These records currently held.

In addition to the above, Ritchie was awarded British vests every year from 1990 to 1995; was the British 24-hour Champion in 1990, 1991, 1992 and 1994; the 100 km Champion in 1990 and 1992; and European 100 km Veterans Champion in 1992.

He was awarded Scottish vests in 1983, 1985, 1987, 1990 and 1994; and set the Lands End to John o' Groats solo record in 1989 (10 days 15 hours 25 minutes).

BOWLING

A bowling postie: 1980s–90s

Richard Corsie, originally from Edinburgh, has won many trophies since becoming Scottish Junior Bowls Champion in 1983.

Equally at home on indoor carpet or outdoor, Corsie has picked up six world titles (in both singles and pairs), a Commonwealth gold in the singles in 1994 plus many other prestigious victories.

Scots champions on the green rinks: Indoor Bowling Championships, 1980s–2003

Since the World Indoor Bowling Championships were inaugurated in 1979, several Scots, both male and female, have won titles in the event:

Singles (Men): 1982, John Watson; 1983, Bob Sutherland; 1988, Hugh Duff; 1989, Richard Corsie; 1990, Richard Corsie; 1993, Richard Corsie; 1996, David Gourlay Jnr; 1997, Hugh Duff; 1998, Paul Foster; 1999, Alex Marshall; 2000, Paul Foster; 2003, Alex Marshall.

Doubles: 1994, Alex Marshall/ Richard Corsie; 1998, Graham Robertson/ Richard Corsie; 1999, David Gourlay/ Alex Marshall; 2001, Hugh Duff/ Paul Foster.

Singles (Women): 1992, Sarah Gourlay; 1993, Kate Adams; 1994, Jan Woodley; 1995, Joyce Lindores; 1998, C McAllister; 1999, C McAllister; 2000, Betty Brown.

Two-Wood Mixed Pairs: 2002, Julie Forrest/Mark Johnston.

The World Bowls Championships, 1966–2004

The World Bowls Championships were first held in 1966 at Kymeemagh, Sydney, New South Wales, Australia. Sixteen countries took part – Australia, Canada, England, Fiji, Hong Kong, Ireland, Jersey,

Kenya, Malawi, New Zealand, Papua New Guinea, Rhodesia (now Zimbabwe), Scotland, South Africa, the USA and Wales. By 2004, that figure had risen to twenty-four.

The country which gains most points in the event gains the Leonard Trophy.

Results

1972, Worthing, England: Scotland won the Leonard Trophy, thanks to these placings: Singles – R. Bernard (2nd); Fours – Scotland (2nd).

1980, Melbourne, Australia: Scotland 3rd overall.

1984, Aberdeen, Scotland: Scotland won the Leonard Trophy: Singles – Willie Wood (2nd); Triples – Scotland (2nd); Fours – Scotland (3rd).

1988, Auckland, New Zealand: Scotland 3rd overall.

1992, Worthing, England: Scotland won the Leonard Trophy: Singles – Richard Corsie (2nd): Pairs – Scotland (1st) R. Corsie/A. Marshall; Triples – Scotland (3rd); Fours – Scotland (1st) G. Robertson/ A. Marshall/ W. Wood/A. Blair.

1996, Adelaide, Australia: Scotland won the Leonard Trophy: Singles – R. Corsie (3rd); Pairs – Scotland (2nd); Triples – Scotland (3rd).

2000, Johannesburg, South Africa: Scotland 2nd overall.

2004, Ayr, Scotland: Scotland won the Leonard Trophy; the host country finished level with New Zealand on 87 points, but took the title with a far superior shots aggregate: Singles – Alex Marshall (2nd); Triples – Scotland beat New Zealand 15–11 in final.

BOXING

A true champion: Ken Buchanan, 1960s–80s

Ken Buchanan was born in Edinburgh and turned professional in 1965. He won both the Scottish and British lightweight titles before heading abroad to gain more recognition.

In 1970 Buchanan travelled to Madrid in a bid to capture the European crown, but lost to Miguel Valasquez. Later that year, though, he conquered the world.

In Puerto Rico, on 26 September 1970, he challenged Ismael Laguna for the world title. The temperature inside the Hiram Bithorn Stadium rose to around the 100-degree mark as the two stars put on a great exhibition of the noble art. Buchanan had the champion in trouble in the 12th round and eventually won the crown on a narrow split decision, two judges going with the Scot 145–144 and the other for the Panamanian by the same score.

In 1971, Buchanan successfully defended his title twice, winning 15-round decisions over Ruben Navarro in Los Angeles and Laguna again at Madison Square Garden in New York. A year later, he returned to the Garden for his most controversial contest.

On 26 June 1972 Buchanan put his title on the line against Panama's Roberto Duran. Duran controlled much of the fight but appeared to throw a low punch in the 13th round; the Scot complained to the referee, who said he did not see the infringement, and the fight was stopped before the start of the 14th round.

Three months later, Buchanan stopped Carlos Ortiz in 6 rounds. In 1973, he outpointed Jim Watt to regain the British lightweight title; but, in 1975, he lost in his only other world-title bid, beaten by WBC champion Ishimatsu Suzuki.

In a career lasting from 1965 to 1983. Ken Buchanan had a total of 70 bouts, of which he won 62 (28 by knock-out), with 8 drawn. In 2000 he was inducted to the International Boxing Hall of Fame.

Boxing shorts

When Benny Lynch won the flyweight title, he became the ninth British-born boxer to become a World Boxing Champion.

Lynch's fight with Jackie Brown on 9 May 1935 had the fifth-highest number of knock-downs in a world-title fight.

And when Jackie Paterson beat Peter Keane for the world title in 1943 it was the fifth-quickest time ever, in 61 seconds.

First of the 'Heavies' to visit Scotland: James J. Corbett, 1890s

The first heavyweight boxing champion to visit Scotland was James J. Corbett. Corbett had beaten John L. Sullivan in 1892 for the Championship but his visit had nothing to do with boxing.

He had come to Scotland to appear in the melodrama *Gentleman Jack,* staged in the Royal Lyceum Theatre in Edinburgh between 28 and 31 May 1895. The play was described in an evening paper as a 'large tax on the public patience'.

Johnny Hill: boxing world–title contender, 1929

Johnny Hill, from Strathmiglo, was the first Scot to be named as a boxing world-title contender.

Hill won the European Flyweight Championship in 1929, a feat not equalled until Pat Clinton lifted the same title in 1990. However, while in training for a fight with US contender Frankie Gennaro in 1930, Johnny Hill took ill and died shortly afterwards.

Our first world boxing champion: Benny Lynch, 1930s

It was on 9 September 1935 that Benny Lynch blasted his way into Scotland's sporting history. In the Belle Vue arena in Manchester that night, the wee man from the Gorbals in Glasgow won the World, European and British flyweight championships when he beat the holder, local man Jackie Brown, the end coming 1 minute and 42 seconds into the second round, after Brown had been floored eight times!

Curiously enough, Lynch's win was not the lead story in the following day's papers. The shooting of the controversial American politician, Senator Huey Long was the big talking point on the front pages but Lynch certainly took up the back page and several before it. He came home to a hero's welcome and Glasgow and Scotland belonged to Benny Lynch.

The champion then made two successful defences of his title, firstly knocking out Londoner Pat Palmer at Shawfield Stadium on 16 September 1936; and secondly out-pointing the American Small Montana, at Wembley Stadium on 19 January 1937, when he received £2600 for his night's work.

Later that same year came the fight which caught the attention of the east of Glasgow, the clash between Lynch and Pat Kane, which the press talked up for some weeks before the fight. The *Daily Record* even signed up the British heavyweight star Tommy Farr to cover the contest and he was joined at the ringside by film star Victor McLaglen.

The fight lived up to its billing. Farr described it as 'one of the greatest ring battles ever fought in Scotland. The fight will go down in history as an epic.' And Lynch won by knocking out Kane in the 13th round. Benny was on top of the world.

However, a more insidious opponent began to take over his life. Everyone wanted to get a piece of him; in every hotel, they swarmed up to him, wanting to shake his hand, have their photograph taken with him, buy him a drink. Benny was particularly happy to accept the latter; after all, what harm could a wee dram do to a world champion?

The problem was, the drink might not do much damage to a champion in full training, but Lynch was neglecting that part of his routine. At the weigh-in for his next defence, on 29 June 1938, he stepped on the scales at a massive six and one-half pounds over the stipulated eight stone. The authorities had no alternative but to strip Lynch of his titles.

The fight went ahead, as a non-title bout, and Lynch knocked out his opponent, Jackie Jurich of America, in the twelfth round. Jurich, though, went off with the title. Lynch's career went downhill from then on. He had one or two attempts to make a comeback, without being able either to keep his weight under control or maintain his fitness, and he gradually slipped out of the public's consciousness, until a dramatic announcement in the papers of 7 August 1946:

> Benny Lynch died suddenly in the Southern General Hospital, Glasgow, last night. He was taken to the hospital shortly after five o'clock and three hours later succumbed to his illness. He was 33 years of age and is survived by his wife and two children. Just over a week ago Benny Lynch fought in a boxing booth in Glasgow Green.

Scotland's second world boxing champion: Jackie Paterson, 1940s

Jackie Paterson won the world flyweight title on 19 June 1943 when he defeated Peter Kane in just 61 seconds at Hampden Park. Paterson was a corporal in the RAF during the Second World War. In 1946 he defended his title against Liverpool's Joe Curran again at Hampden, before 45,000. But now his weight began to be a problem and he lost the title to Rinty Monaghan in Belfast in 1948. Tragically, Jackie Paterson lost his life after being stabbed by a broken bottle in South Africa in 1966.

Scottish losers in boxing, 1920s–60s

In the days when there were only eight weight categories in professional boxing, several Scots fought – and failed – to win world-title bouts.

In 1927, at 29 years of age, and holder of the British and European flyweight titles, Elky Clark travelled to New York to fight Italian-American Fidel La Barba on 21 January in Madison Square Garden. The fight was over the unusual distance of twelve rounds, and although Clark suffered severe eye damage early on, he bravely battled on but lost on points. Shortly afterwards Clark lost the sight of that eye.

Later that same year, on 30 June, it was the turn of Lanarkshire's Tommy Milligan to fight for a world title. He took a fairly short trip to London, to meet the American champion Mickey Walker over fifteen rounds for the world middleweight crown. Milligan's defeat in the tenth round made front-page news.

Then, in January 1952, in Johannesburg, South Africa, Peter Keenan lost his chance to become world bantamweight champion when he was beaten on points by Vic Toweel.

And in October 1966, in San Juan, Chic Calderwood lost a world light-heavyweight clash to the Puerto Rican Jose Torres, the Scot being knocked out in the second round. Tragically, one month later, Calderwood was killed in a car crash back in his native country.

The battle of Annandale Street, 1942

Fortunately, riots and disturbances at sporting events in Scotland are relatively rare. They certainly did occur at different times in our history and one or two are covered elsewhere in this book; but compared to the number of events, they were not the norm.

Yet, on 26 November 1924, as 20,000 fans screamed themselves hoarse inside a major boxing venue, thousands more outside fought a running battle with baton-wielding policemen.

Annandale Street leads off Leith Walk, heading towards Powderhall Stadium. Back in the 1920s, about halfway along the street, stood the Industrial Hall, a large red-brick building topped with glass domes. On that particular Wednesday in 1924, it staged the first British and European welterweight fight ever held in Scotland.

The protagonists were top men. The defending champion was Ted 'Kid' Lewis, from London. Born Gershom Mendlehoff in London's East End, Lewis had fought a number of times for the World Championship and was also the first fighter to wear a gumshield. Normally, he would not have come north for such a fight but Lewis had been having financial problems and welcomed any opportunity for a pay-day.

His opponent was Tommy Milligan, the undoubted star of the 'Hamilton School' of boxers, managed by Paddy McGreechan and trained by Tommy Murphy. This was a most important fight for the Lanarkshire boy in a career that would eventually lead him to a tilt at Mickey Walker's world title and he had prepared with more than normal dedication.

Once the fight got under way, it was noticeable that Lewis looked drawn and lifeless. Not only was he much the older man but he was now having trouble making the welterweight limit of 10 stone 7 pounds. Eventually, Milligan took the verdict on points.

Unfortunately, while a capacity crowd watched the action inside the building, many more were gathered outside and many had tickets for the fight. They charged the doors, trying to get in, and eventually a barrier gave way. The police responded to force with force, with many fans struck by batons as they tried to push their way in.

Both sides were blamed afterwards for the trouble but the real culprit got off relatively lightly. The London Midland and Scottish Railway Company had guaranteed to take thousands of Lanarkshire fight fans through to Edinburgh and promised that they would be there on time. This did not happen, and by the time many of these fans reached the stadium they could not get in, even when they showed the tickets they had bought. The promotors had also provided a pay-at-the-door system and many of those inside were taking the places of those who had bought tickets.

In sporting terms, Milligan may have beaten Lewis, but when people talk about the Battle of Annandale Street they are more likely to be referring to the one outside the ring.

The day an Italian Alp came to Edinburgh: Primo Carnera, 1929

A huge crowd had gathered at Waverley Station on a chilly November afternoon in 1929 to await the arrival of the London express. Some were dressed in the casual fashion of the times, others were more formally attired. There was even a group of men wearing black shirts as a form of uniform. As the train came to a stop, they all rushed forward, keen to get close to the man they all wanted to see. Suddenly, the carriage door opened and, to a sudden silence, Primo Carnera emerged on to the platform.

Known as the 'Ambling Alp', 'Satchel Feet', or the '20th-Century Colussus', Primo Carnera had been born near Venice and was a circus strongman when discovered by his manager Leon See. See taught his new charge the rudiments of boxing and took him on a tour through Europe and Britain, where he certainly drew the crowds.

At a time when the average heavyweight boxing champion was around the 14-stone mark, Carnera weighed in at 19 stone 4 pounds and scaled 6 feet 5 inches! The crowd already knew the details of his height and weight but were so stunned by seeing him in the flesh that the initial reaction was one of astonishment. And Carnera's immediate gesture of a fascist salute did nothing to improve their response, although the delighted Italian Consul and his black-shirted colleagues were quick to rush forward and shake his hand.

After exchanging a few words with the Consul and his supporters, Carnera and his manager fell in behind a pipe band from Dr Guthrie's Industrial School, who led a procession along Princes Street to the Caledonian Hotel.

However, the 'Italian Alp' had little time to admire the view from his hotel, as he was whisked by car to Glasgow to box some exhibition bouts with, among others, Bobby Sheilds, heavyweight champion of Scotland.

Two days later, Carnera sparred at the Marine Gardens in Portobello with other Scots stars, including Tommy Milligan, Tom Berry and Tancy Lee. The massive Italian wore 20-ounce 'pillow' gloves for these so-called contests, but unfortunately they were neither a fistic nor a financial success. Scottish fight fans recognised the venture for what it was; they much preferred a real fight. Even the boxing correspondent of the *Edinburgh Evening Dispatch* described the shows as 'nicely staged burlesque'.

Thus ended Primo Carnera's first trip to Scotland.

Within the following few years, manager Leon See was deposed by the New York mobster Owney Madden, under whose 'guidance' the Italian boxer won the world heavyweight boxing championship. However, in spite of several contests against big names like Joe Louis and Maxie Baer, Carnera by 1939 was abandoned, alone and in a New York hospital. He even had to return to Italy by cattle-boat.

This tale has a happy ending, though. After the war, Primo Carnera turned to wrestling, whose contrived atmosphere he found much more to his liking. Indeed he told reporters on his second visit to Edinburgh in 1960 that it provided a lucrative living, enabling him to put his son through university and train as a dentist.

Primo Carnera might not have been the best boxer ever to have visited Scotland but he was certainly the biggest!

The last of the few: Jim Watt, 1979–80

Jim Watt was the last Scottish boxer to win an undisputed world title.

After Roberto Duran left the world lightweight championship vacant in 1979, the World Boxing Council nominated Watt as a contender and also put up Columbia's Alfredo Pitalua. The pair met at the Kelvin Hall in Glasgow on 18 April of that year and Watt wrapped up the title by stopping Pitalua in the 12th round.

Watt certainly kept himself busy. On 9 November 1979, he beat American Robert Vasquez in Glasgow, the referee stopping the contest in the 9th round. In March of the following year he needed only four rounds to dispose of Ireland's Charlie Nash; a few months later he had a points victory over the highly regarded American Howard Davis; he then defeated the Irish-American challenger Sean O'Grady in a controversial fight, where O'Grady's corner claimed that the eye wound of their man – which stopped the fight proceeding beyond the 12th round – was caused by a head butt. The referee did not agree with their thoughts and awarded Watt the decision. However, at Wembley Stadium, in June 1980, Jim Watt lost his title when he was outpointed by the very talented Nicaraguan, Alexis Arguello.

For his efforts in the ring, Watt received the MBE and now makes his living as a boxing summariser and after-dinner speaker

———

Since the early 1980s several different organizations have started up in boxing, all of which have their own versions of the world title at an increasing number of weight categories. Four Scots have won world titles as follows: Murray Sutherland, IBF, Super-middleweight, 1984; Pat

Clinton, WBO Flyweight, 1992; Paul Weir, WBO Mini-flyweight, 1992; Scott Harrison, WBO Featherweight, 2003.

Most unusually, both Clinton and Weir lost their titles to the same man, Baby Jake Matlala of South Africa.

The only amateur Scot to win the big prize: Dick McTaggart, 1950s–60s

Dick McTaggart took part in a remarkable 634 fights in his amateur career but none matched up to the one in Melbourne on the first Monday of December 1956, when he became the first Scot to win an Olympic gold medal.

After leaving school, McTaggart, one of five Dundee brothers, started work as a butcher, spending his spare time improving his boxing skills.

These were already considerable and further practice made him an assured competitor. A stint in the RAF, where he trained as a cook, improved his fitness, and by the time he travelled with the GB contingent to Australia, his hopes were high.

After three fairly easy victories in Melbourne, McTaggart had a difficult time in the final against the German, Harry Kurschat, but he worked hard to win the gold medal and the Val Barker Trophy as the best stylist of the Games.

In 1958 he won his second ABA title and took the gold medal at the Commonwealth Games in Cardiff. He picked up another ABA championship in 1960 and also a bronze medal in the Rome Olympics, losing out to the eventual winner, Kamizierz Pazdior of Poland, in the semi-final.

By 1962, McTaggart had moved up to light-welterweight and won silver at the Commonwealth Games in Perth, Australia. Two years later, he became the only British boxer to compete in three Olympics, when he lost in the early rounds in Mexico, again to the eventual winner.

By then, McTaggart's time at the top was drawing to a close but he managed a fifth and final ABA title in 1965 before announcing his retirement. He continued to give good service to the sport and was coach to the Scottish team at the 1990 Commonwealth Games.

Walter McGowan, 1960s

Walter McGowan won the ABA flyweight championship in 1961 before turning professional. In the pro ranks, he got off to a quick start by winning the British and Commonwealth Flyweight Championship when he beat Jackie Brown in Paisley on 2 June 1963, aged 20.

McGowan became world flyweight champion with a fine victory over Salvatore Burrundi at the Empire Pool in London in June 1966. In the first defence of that title, later that same year, McGowan met Chartchai Chionoi of Thailand in Bangkok. The Scot fought well but a cut across the bridge of his nose in the second round refused to stop bleeding and the fight was eventually stopped in the ninth round.

Moving up a weight, McGowan defeated Alan Rudkin for the British and Commonwealth bantamweight title in September 1967.

Why should a world heavyweight boxing champion want to come to Scotland?

When fight fans throughout the world meet to discuss the various issues in boxing, it is almost inevitable that they get round to arguing over the best heavyweights of all time. Everyone has their own personal favourites, like Mohammed Ali, Joe Louis or Rocky Marciano, but you can also be sure that the name of Jack Johnson rates highly in their eyes.

The son of an illiterate woodcutter, John Arthur Johnson was born in Galveston, Texas in 1878 and ran away from home at the age of 12 to work in a racing stable. During his teenage years, he became too big for any future in that field, switched to boxing, and by time he was 19 he had moved into the professional ranks.

For years, he fought to become the main challenger for the World Championship, but his ambitions were always thwarted, often on grounds of racial prejudice. Eventually, he almost stalked the title-holder, Tommy Burns, catching up with him in Sydney, Australia, where Johnson's taunts of cowardice got under the champion's skin and he agreed to meet the American on 30 December 1908.

For the 14 rounds of the fight, Johnson, 6 inches taller and 20 pounds heavier, treated Burns as his plaything before police intervened to save him. Jack Johnson thus became the heavyweight champion of the world. He also became the most hated black man in America, not just for being the first black champion, anathema to many whites, but also because he refused to accept the normal status of a negro at that time.

In fact, he rather flaunted his position, becoming boastful and arrogant, driving round in top-range cars and having a succession of white girlfriends. But why did he want to come to Scotland in October 1911?

Well, after he had beaten Jim Jeffries in Reno, Nevada, in 1910, another of the black–white confrontations which led to race riots, Johnson travelled to Britain to fulfil a series of 'theatrical engagements'. In Newcastle upon Tyne one night, he happened to mention to a fellow performer that he had always wanted to be a Freemason, but no Lodge in America would admit him. Recently, that desire had intensified, as his wife's father was high up in the Masonic Order back in the States.

The actor he had spoken to happened to be a member of a Scottish Lodge and he sent a telegram to the secretary, explaining Johnson's position and request. By return of post, the world champion received a cordial invitation to be inducted into the first degree of Freemasonry by Lodge Forfar and Kincardine at the Meadow Street Hall.

Johnson and his wife arrived in Dundee on 13 October 1911. He was initiated in comparative peace but, as he returned to his hotel, the Royal, he was overwhelmed by the locals, all wanting to shake the hand of the champion.

Yet, as an obviously happy Johnson left for the return trip to England, questions were being raised by the Grand Lodge committee in Edinburgh and eventually the Dundee officials were summoned to explain their actions. It was stressed that the doubts about their actions were not based on grounds of race but of procedure.

The result of the inquiry was announced in the *Dundee Advertiser* on 20 April 1912; 'Jack Johnson the champion pugilist of the world admitted to the company of Dundee Freemasons by Lodge Forfar and Kincardine of the craft. But objection having been taken, his invitation was declared null and void by Grand Lodge of Scotland.'

We don't know Jack Johnson's reaction but he must have been disappointed by the events. No doubt the Grand Lodge committee members were correct to follow the rules of procedure, but I should imagine that Johnson, with his background and awareness of the position of the black man in American society, must have wondered if Scotland was any better?

CLIMBING

A Scotswoman on top of the world

On the second weekend of May 2004, a sudden improvement of the weather conditions in the Himalayas allowed 30 mountaineers and 29 Sherpas to climb Everest, the world's highest mountain.

Among them was 51-year-old Vicky Jack, from Perthshire, who became the oldest British woman to have conquered the peak. At the same time, she became the first Scotswoman to climb the highest mountains of each of the world's seven continents: Europe: Mt Elbrus, Georgia, 18,510 feet; Africa: Mt Kilimanjaro, Tanzania, 19,340 feet; South America: Anconcagua, Argentina, 22,843 feet; Antarctica: Mt Vinson, 16,023 feet; Asia: Mt Everest, Nepal, 29,029 feet; North America: Mt McKinley, Alaska, 20,320 feet; Australasia: Mt Carstenz, Indonesia, 16,024 feet.

The first Munroist: Revd Archibald Eneas Robertson, 1901

Towards the end of the 19th century, a very keen Scottish climber, Sir Hugh Munro, identified around the country 283 peaks of more than 3,000 feet. These soon became known as 'Munros' in his honour.

The first man to climb all 283 was the Revd Archibald Eneas Robertson, born in Helensburgh in 1870. He gained his love for climbing on family holidays on Arran, where he scaled the highest peak on the island, Goat Fell, at the age of 12. By the time he was 20, the mountains had become his passion, a solo walk up Scotland's highest, Ben Nevis, a particular highlight.

Robertson only climbed once in the Alps, when he ascended the Matterhorn and the Rimpfischhorn in 1908, but he preferred 'good, sound Scottish snow'. And it was on the summit of Glencoe's Meall Dearg in 1901, dressed in a heavy woollen cape, tweed jacket, plus fours and hobnailed boots, that he became the first 'Munroist' by kissing both the cairn at the summit and his climbing companion, his wife Kate, before opening a bottle of champagne in celebration.

The first Scot on top of the world: Dougal Haston, 1970

Dougal Haston was born in Currie, West Lothian, in 1940. As a youngster, he developed a taste for climbing, trekking round the hills just outside Edinburgh and climbing up railway and riverside walls around his home town.

An exuberant youth, Haston and his friends would occasionally be the subject of some neighbourly disapproval by climbing to the top of Currie Church, and leaving various items, including ladies' underwear, atop the flagpole. He soon began rock- and ice-climbing, quickly developing a reputation for his talent.

At the age of 26, in 1966, Haston gained fame for the first direct (bottom to top) ascent of the North Face of the Eiger in Switzerland. Tragically, a broken rope cost the life of the American climbing star John Harlin during the ascent, but Haston finished the climb with a group of Germans and named the route John Harlin Direct.

From Europe, Haston graduated to the Himalayas, making the first climb of the South Face of Annapurna in 1970 and the first summit of Changabang in India in 1974. Two years later, along with fellow Briton Doug Scott, Haston became the first Scot to climb Everest, ascending by a previously unused route up the South West Face. The pair were forced by bad weather to huddle in a hand-dug snow cave at the South Summit but emerged unharmed by their experience. Later that same year Haston would participate in the first climb of the south-west face of Mount McKinley in Alaska.

Tragically, Dougal Haston was killed by a minor avalanche near his home in Leysin, Switzerland, in 1977.

CRICKET

The thump of the willow comes to Scotland

The first match played by a representative Scottish XI was in 1865, but the one regarded as Scotland's first-ever first class encounter was against the Australians at Raeburn Place, Edinburgh, from 30 June to 2 July 1905.

For Scotland's first first-class century, cricket lovers had to wait until 1922, when Alexander Fergusson scored 103 over 2 hours 45 minutes against the MCC at Lords, although his team were soundly beaten. The first bowler to take 10 wickets in a match for Scotland was Walter Ringrose, 8 for 86 and 4 for 60 against Nottinghamshire at Raeburn Place in 1908.

Scotland's first score of over 400 was the 485 against Ireland at Perth in 1909; and the first win over an English county came against Warwickshire in 1959.

A cricketer who played rugby, or perhaps vice versa? George McGregor, 1890s

George McGregor (1869–1919) was a wicket-keeper of exceptional ability. At Cambridge, he held his place in the first team for four years, captaining the side to victory over Oxford in his final year.

While still an undergraduate, 'Mac' played for England against Australia, standing up close at the stumps no matter how fast the bowlers. In 1891–92, he toured Australia with Lord Sheffield's side; and he also led Middlesex from 1899 to 1907. All-in, he made 8 test-match appearances.

McGregor's international rugby career started in 1890, when he played in the fullback position against Wales (A), Ireland (H) and England (A). In the following year, against the same three opponents, he had moved to centre. Another six caps were to follow later in the 1890s, including the 11–0 win over England at Old Hampden Park when McGregor once again appeared at fullback

Alma Hunt, 1939

Alma Hunt may not have been a Scot but he did give one of the world's best-ever cricket performances in a Scottish counties match.

It was a fine afternoon in Linlithgow in July 1939 when the Aberdeenshire openers took to the field for a game aginst West Lothian. Before too long, they were back in the pavilion, having scored only 8 and 4; and before much longer they were joined by the rest of the team, as Aberdeenshire crashed to 48 all out.

The West Lothian side had fielded well, although their star was the Bermudan, Alma Hunt. Eight-ball overs were then being tried out and Hunt finished with the splendid fugures of 12.7 overs, 6 maidens, 11 runs, 7 wickets. He took his last 3 wickets in 4 balls.

That might have been enough of a day's work for most players but Hunt was not yet finished. Out he came with T. A. Findlay to open the Aberdeenshire innings and immediately took centre stage, scoring all of the 49 runs in an astonishing knock to give his side victory.

After three overs, he had scored only 7. In the next, he started to pull and drive, picking up 0, 4, 6, 4, 4, 0, 0 and 1 to move on to 26. Off the following over, he got another 5, taking him up to 31; and then, in the next again, he only needed six balls to win the match, hitting 6, 0, 0, 4, 4 and 4.

Seven wickets for 11 runs and then a knock of 49 from 33 balls. If this is not a world record, then there is a really astonishing performance yet to be found.

West Lothian

F.C. Benham	lbw Hunt	8
R.R. Philip	c Melis b Donaldson	4
J. Dumbreck	c Rice b Donaldson	1
A.J. Benham	c Robertson b Hunt	5
A.C. Ford	b Hunt	10
J.H. Mathieson	c Findlay b Catto	8
W. Summerville	b Hunt	1

W. MacKay	not out	2
J. Clarke	b Hunt	5
A.J. Benham	b Hunt	0
J. Smart	b Hunt	0
Extras		*4*
Total		48

Aberdeenshire

A. Hunt	not out	49
T.A. Findlay	not out	0
Extras		*0*
Total		49

Archie Jackson, 1930s

He scored 164 in his first innings in international cricket, for Australia against England in 1929, yet Archibald Alexander Jackson was Scottish.

The third of four children, Archie was born in Rutherglen, in the south-east of Glasgow, in September 1909. Soon afterwards, though, his father Sandy, who had spent some of his formative years Down Under, decided that Australia would be a better place to bring up his family, and they settled in Sydney.

Sport ran in the Jackson family. Sandy's brother James played professional football for more than twenty years with Rangers, Newcastle, Arsenal, West Ham and Greenock Morton. James's son, Jimmy, also joined the pro ranks, playing for Aberdeen before heading to Liverpool, where he became club captain.

Archie Jackson was also a useful footballer but as he lived only 100 yards from the home of Balmain Cricket Club in Sydney, the summer sport caught more of his attention. He made his debut for the club in 1924, only one month after his fifteenth birthday. The rather skinny lad with what looked like over-sized pads and bat may have appeared a figure of fun, but his talent and determination soon caught the respect of the opposition and the watching crowd.

As he developed towards his start for New South Wales in 1926, Jackson came up against another young star, Don Bradman. In fact, at this stage Jackson was probably ahead in terms of development. In that debut for NSW – against Queensland – Jackson got off to a bad start, an attack of nerves causing his dismissal for a duck. However, in the second innings he redeemed himself, making 86.

In the 1928–29 season, England arrived for a test series, showing their dominance by crushing Australia in the first two tests and retaining the Ashes in the third. Apart from the flamboyant Don Bradman, the Australian side was an ageing side; once England had won, the selectors decided to give youth a fling, and Archie Jackson's name was put forward.

On 1 February 1929, at the age of 19 years and 142 days, replying to an England total of 334, Jackson strode out at Adelaide to open Australia's innings. Before long, the home side were on 19 for 3, but Jackson held his form and, with the help firstly of skipper Jack Ryder and then Don Bradman, he made his 100, bringing up the century by driving Harold Larwood for 4.

On a very hot day, he went on to make 164, hammering the English attack all over the field and leaving to a standing ovation. Despite these heroics, Australia lost the fourth and fifth test, but the selectors felt that in Bradman and Jackson they had a platform on which to build for the future.

Unfortunately, ill health suddenly struck Jackson. He had his tonsils removed just before the England tour of the following year and that left him susceptible to infections. On the tour, he struggled to find form, depressed by the cold, damp weather. Jackson took in Wimbledon and even managed a trip to Liverpool to see his cousin Jimmy play. In later life, Jimmy became a minister.

When the Australians came to Scotland, Jackson was not available for the official match at Raeburn Place; a few days later, though, he was delighted to play at Hamilton Crescent in Glasgow, not too far from his birthplace. Out of form, and alongside a dazzling Bradman, Jackson still managed a respectable 52, the crowd good-naturedly barracking their own cricket hero all the way through.

Jackson missed the fourth test but came back for the fifth at the Oval, where he and Bradman made a vital stand of 243 to help Australia regain the Ashes by an innings and 39 runs. The following year, Jackson played four tests against the West Indies, but by now severe bouts of ill health had become a common occurrence, and in 1932 he was admitted to a sanatorium, where TB was diagnosed. He spent the winter of 1932 in Sydney, then moved to Brisbane the following summer, much against doctors' orders. The warm, humid climate of Queensland was not regarded as appropriate for a TB sufferer.

Jackson collapsed on 10 February 1933, during the fourth test against England. Five days later he died; he was twenty-four years of age.

Jackson' Record: Tests, 8; Innings, 11; Not Outs, 1; Highest Score, 164; Runs, 474; Average, 47.40.

A 'Scottish' England cricket captain: Mike Denness, 1950–80s

Although it is now played world-wide, the game of cricket is quintessentially English in its origins and traditions.

Certainly, the game began in England in the 18th century; developed into a spectator sport in the 19th, when the English County Championship was formed; and has had the frequent clashes between England and Australia (first one in 1877) as one of its highlights.

Imagine, then, the consternation of many cricket-lovers south of the Border when a Scotsman captained the English team in the 1970s?

Mike Denness had been an outstanding schoolboy player at Ayr Academy and made his debut for Scotland in 1959. By 1962 he had moved south to Kent, where he was awarded his county cap three years later, forming a successful opening partnership with Brian Luckhurst.

Eventually, Denness became Kent captain, having outstanding success, notably in one-day cricket. He brought a great deal of soundness and enthusiasm to the job, setting a great example to his team-mates through some excellent fielding. Unfortunately, his strong outer demeanour covered a shy and sensitive nature, one not suited to the PR demands of press and TV.

Denness played his first match for England against New Zealand at the Oval during the third test in 1969; was vice-captain on the tour of India, Pakistan and Sri Lanka in 1972–73; and went on to make 28 test-match appearances, in 19 of which he was captain, scoring 1,667 runs (36.69) in total.

In 1977, Denness moved to Essex, where he played a pivotal role in the county's two competition wins in 1979. He went on to work in insurance, finance and public relations and as a manager for World Series teams. From 1981 to 1984 he was coach of the Essex 2nd XI, and he became an honorary life member of the MCC.

Cricket Scots prove to be the best: the village of Freuchie, 1985

The official title of the competition is the National Village Cricket Championship. South of the Border, though, it is usually referred to as the English Village Cricket Championship. Either way, a Scots team won it in 1985.

The village of Freuchie lies a few miles north of Glenrothes, in the county of Fife. In the mid-1980s the population was 1,746. A feature of the village was the local cricket club, at that time a low white building with a bar and a view over the pitch. In 1985, the club, along with more than 630 others scattered throughout the land, entered the National Village Cricket Championship. They did well, eventually reaching the final, played at Lords on 31 August.

Half the village made the pilgrimage to the home of cricket and stamped their presence on the ground. To a specially composed tune – 'Freuchie's March to Lords' – Pipe-major Alistair Pirnie led the team through the Grace Gates and on to the field, cheered all the way by their loyal fans.

It turned out to be a close match with a dramatic finale. Both teams scored 134 runs, but while Freuchie's Surrey opponents were all out, the Scots still had two wickets in hand and took the trophy north of the Border for the first time.

Scotland stumped: Hugo Yarnold, 1951

For Scots cricket fans, the match between Scotland and Worcestershire, at Broughty Ferry in the summer of 1951, entered the record books for all the wrong reasons.

Scotland batted first, when the Revd Aitchison of Kilmarnock batted for all but 10 minutes of the innings, making 64 out of a poor tally of

114. At one point, when they were on 121 for 5, Worcestershire's reply did not look promising either. However, at the start of the second day, the Ceylonese all-rounder, Laddie Outschoorn, showed his class and raced away to an unbeaten 200. This allowed the English side to declare at 351 for 9, giving them a first-innings lead of 237.

Worcestershire's second-highest score, 46, came from wicket-keeper 'Hugo' Yarnold, batting at number 8. He had 1 stumping in Scotland's first innings and now, as the opening twosome came to start the second, he took his place behind the stumps.

Scotland had their opening bat, R.H. Chisholm, out for 15, then I. Anderson and the Revd Aitchison put on 79 for the second wicket. A good ball by Bradley tempted Anderson into an injudicious shot and Yarnold took a good catch. The wicket-keeper, just about to celebrate his thirty-fourth birthday, then proceeded to pick up the next six batsmen too – all by stumpings!

Not all the credit should go to Yarnold, though, as obviously the bowlers played their part. Roly Jenkins used a combination of leg-breaks and googlies to bemuse the Scottish batsmen; while Bradley, an orthodox left-hander, plugged away on a good length.

However, six stumpings in one innings cannot be put down merely to luck, and Hugo Yarnold deserves great credit for his accuracy, timing and swiftness.

Scotland

R.H.E Chisholm	b Jenkins	17	c Whiting b Jenkins	15
I. Anderson	b Hughes	0	c Yarnold b Bradley	40
J. Aitchison	hit wkt b Bradley	64	st Yarnold b Bradley	44
J.D. Henderson	b Jenkins	7	st Yarnold b Jenkins	23
N.G. Davidson	b Perks	9	st Yarnold b Bradley	7
F.O. Thomas	st Yarnold b Jenkins	0	st Yarnold b Jenkins	21
S.H.Cosh	b Perks	3	st Yarnold b Jenkins	8
D.W. Drummond	c Dews b Bradley	10	b Whiting	15
A.M. Dowell	not out	1	st Yarnold b Jenkins	2
J.H. Allan	c Richardson b Jenkins	0	b Whiting	0
G.W. Youngson	b Jenkins	3	not out	0
Extras		3		12
Total		114		187

Worcestershire

Cooper	c Cosh b Dowell	7
P Richardson b Dowell		21
Outschoorn	not out	200
Broadbent	run out	15
Dews	c Allan B Youngson	4
Whiting	b Youngson	0
Jenkins	b Youngson	19
Yarnold	lbw b Allan	46
Parks	c Anderson b Allan	12
Hughes	b Allan	10
Bradley	not out	6
Extras		*11*
Total		351 for 9 declared

West of Scotland Cricket Ground, Hamilton Crescent, Partick

There can be few sporting venues in Scotland with such a rich history as West of Scotland Cricket Ground at Hamilton Crescent, Partick, on the west side of Glasgow just north of the River Clyde.

The club was founded in 1862 by local businessmen and players from the Clutha Cricket Club, who had been using the northern part of Hamilton Crescent for matches. All-England elevens were invited to play at the ground and the first Australian cricket team to visit Scotland played there in 1878. In 1891 a team led by the famous Dr W.G. Grace beat West of Scotland by an innings and 33 runs.

On 30 November 1872, a football match was the subject of much attention, when 4,000 turned up to see the first Scotland versus England international, which resulted in a 0–0 draw. The club received the sum of one pound ten shillings (£1.50) for the hire of the ground. The following two home fixtures against England were also held there.

In 1874, 7,000 were present to see Scotland win 2–1, thanks to goals by Anderson (Clydesdale) and McKinnon (Queen's Park). And in 1876, goals by McKinnon and Highet (Queen's Park) gave Scotland a 3–0 victory, to the delight of the 16,000 crowd.

When a whole team was out for a duck, 1960

When we take into account the weather in this country, it is perhaps surprising that we play cricket at all. Yet there is a whole host of clubs devoted to the game, with many more people entranced by the whole spectacle of a match.

A few have to go to extreme lengths for a game – like the players of Ross County, for instance. In the North of Scotland League, they can sometimes travel between 100 and 200 miles to an away match.

In May 1964, only 10 players turned up for a match at Elgin, but they decided to travel anyway. Elgin batted first, reached the respectable total of 145 for 5, and then declared to give their pace attack of Woolfson and Murray the advantage of good conditions.

Woolfson took two wickets with his first two deliveries. Murray's opening over also claimed one victim. With his first ball of the new over, Woolfson dismissed Ross County's no. 4 batsman; no. 5 went out to the fourth; no. 6 to the sixth ball.

Murray then took control and claimed wickets with his third, fourth and final deliveries to finish the match. Ross County were all out for no runs.

Observers noted that they had had little luck. One batsman had hit his own wicket; two others had played on to their stumps; they had no run of the ball ... but no runs either!

Elgin

T. Manley	b Oliver	28
B. Woolfson	b Hendry	0
J. Wright	b Nevin	43
F. Muir	lbw b Nevin	8
J. Leithhead	not out	36
W. Ohimister	b Nevin	6
R. Fraggan	not out	12
Extras		*12*
Total (for 5 wickets)		145

Ross County

B. Kenney	c Phimister b Woolfson	0
G. Shiels	c Stewardson b Murray	0
J. Hendry	b Woolfson	0
W. Oliver	b Woolfson	0
J. Nevin	hit wicket b Murray	0
R. Hannant	lbw b Woolfson	0
I. Taylor	b Woolfson	0
S. Bull	not out	0

J. Northcliffe	b Murray	0
N. Frazer	b Murray	0
Extras		*0*
Total		0

Before this match, other Scottish teams had held the record for the lowest score in an innings. In 1896, for instance, Kinross had scored one against Auchtermuchty; while in 1968, Arbroath United had been all out for two against Aberdeen. But nobody can ever beat the record held by Ross County. They could only equal it.

FOOTBALL

A bad day at the office: Bobby Houston, 1978

A day which had started promisingly for Bobby Houston was beginning to deteriorate.

Shortly after being transferred by Partick Thistle to Kilmarnock in 1978, he was due to play against his former club at Rugby Park and was keen to show that they were wrong to let him go. As he hit the pillow on the Friday evening, his thoughts were concentrated on the game and more importantly, his part in it.

However, on the morning of the match, things started going wrong. Breakfasting late, he dressed casually before heading off for a haircut to 'smarten himself up'. A combination of a busy hairdresser and heavy traffic left him with no time to reach home again and change, so he had to travel to the match in his T-shirt and jeans.

This did not please the Kilmarnock management, who were quick to rap Bobby over the knuckles; and he was further aggrieved to find out he had been named as a substitute. When the Thistle bus arrived, he went out to speak to his old mates, but, unknown to him, they had agreed – as a joke – to ignore 'Badger' (as Bobby was known). Guys like Colin McAdam and Brian Whittaker pushed past him as if he didn't exist.

All through the first half, a very angry Bobby Houston sat on the bench, but shortly after the interval he was called into the fray. As he passed the Thistle bench, their manager, Bertie Auld, made some witty comment, stinging Bobby into a reply. No sooner was he on the pitch than he attempted a very crude tackle on Whittaker, which fortunately missed its target.

Just behind him, his former team-mate Ian Gibson shouted 'What are you doing?' Bobby swung round and threw a punch, which missed. Gibson laughed and Bobby swung again, but the referee and a linesman stepped in to quell further trouble and Bobby was ordered off.

The club was not amused, fining him £40 plus a week's wages, while the SFA banned him for two weeks – a tough sentence in those days.

Bobby Houston looks back on the day and winces at his reckless actions. It was completely out of character for this fine player to get involved in such moments, and he is at pains to stress that kids should learn the right lesson from the incident – never lose your temper on the pitch.

However, the scenario remains one of the most unusual in the history of Scottish football, with Houston surely the only player ever to have been ordered off without touching the ball.

A European Footballer of the Year in Scotland

So far, George Best is the only European Footballer of the Year (won in 1968) to have played for a Scottish club. Best joined Hibs in late 1979 and made a few appearances during the following year.

A lone Scot ... on film, John Wark, 1980s

Films about football have never shown up too well on the big screen. One of the most unusual, *Escape to Victory*, set in a prisoner of war camp in Germany, starred Michael Caine and Sylvester Stallone.

A whole squad of players was brought in to play other parts. Among names like Pele, Bobby Moore and Ossie Ardiles, there was one Scot, John Wark of Ipswich Town.

A referee who did not know the rules

In a second-round tie in the European Cup-Winners' Cup in season 1971/72, Rangers had been drawn against Sporting Lisbon of Portugal, with the first leg set for Ibrox.

Before a crowd of 50,000, the Light Blues went quickly into a 3–0 lead, completely outplaying the Portuguese side, and kept the lead until the interval. In the second period, though, for some reason, they took their collective foot off the pedal and the visitors pulled the score back to 3–2, much to the disgust of the home support.

That did not look too secure a lead to take to Portugal and obviously the Sporting fans thought so too, as over 60,000 packed into the Jose Alavalade Stadium in the Portuguese capital to see the action. Rangers had not had the best of preparations, as an air-traffic control strike in London meant they arrived in Lisbon only 24 hours before the match. Nevertheless, they produced one of the club's best-ever displays in Europe that night.

Twice Rangers came from behind, did well to control the play in the second half and at 5–4 with only minutes left, looked well on course for victory. Then Gomez popped up to score with a header and the teams went into extra-time.

Willie Henderson scored a vital goal but Sporting rallied again, scored through Perez and the match finished at 6–6, with Rangers going through on the away-goals rule. And that was the view of everyone – except Dutch referee Leo Horn. In spite of regulations which clearly stated that away goals should count double to decide drawn ties, he decreed that penalty kicks should be taken.

This was won by Sporting but the official UEFA observer intervened, pointed out the regulations to the referee, who apologised – and awarded the tie to Rangers!

A scoring machine: Jimmy McGrory, 1920s–60s

Jimmy McGrory joined Celtic Football Club from St Roch's Juniors in 1921 at the age of 17.

For the first few months of his professional career he was farmed out to Clydebank but then returned to Celtic Park, where he went on to stamp his name in the record books. During the years between 1923 and 1937, McGrory played 445 matches for Celtic, scoring an astonishing 472 goals, winning League Championship and Scottish Cup medals, yet only gaining a miserly 7 caps for the national team.

After a short spell with Kilmarnock as manager, McGrory returned to Celtic Park in the same role and held the post from 1945 to 1965. He was only the third Celtic manager since the club was founded in 1887.

A Scots team ... in the Bible? Queen of the South

They might not have one of the best records in Scottish football but the 'Doonhammers', or Queen of the South to use the proper title, is the only team to be mentioned in the Bible.

In the Gospel of St Luke in the New Testament, Chaper 11, verse 31, it states; 'The Queen of the South shall rise up in the judgment with the men of this generation, and will condemn them.'

A season to remember for the Wee Rovers

In the first full season after First World War, Albion Rovers had a season to remember. Unfortunately, there were both good moments and bad moments.

In the league campaign, with 22 teams involved, Albion Rovers finished bottom, propping up the table with the following record;

P	W	D	L	F	A	Pts
42	10	8	24	42	77	28

Not a good set of figures. And yet the same team also reached the final of the Scottish Cup, knocking out some big names on the way:

First Round:	24.1.20	Dykehead (H) 0–0	10,000 crowd
	31.1.20 replay	Dykehead (A) 1–0	4,000
Second Round:	7.2.20 w/o	Huntingtower scratched	
Third Round:	21.2.20	St Bernard's (A) 1–1	20,000
	25.2.20 replay	St Bernard's (H) 4–1	10,000
Fourth Round:	6.3.20	Aberdeen (H) 2–1	12,000
Semi-final	27.3.20	Rangers (Celtic Park) 1–1	32,000
	31.3.20 replay	Rangers (Celtic Park) 0–0	37,000
	7.4.20 2nd replay	Rangers (Celtic Park) 2–0	53,000

A long convoluted journey to the final, where their opponents would be Kilmarnock. Curiously, without the presence of either half of the Old Firm, it attracted the biggest attendance thus far for a Scottish Cup final, 95,000 packing into Hampden on 17 April. Unfortunately for the Wee Rovers, on the day Kilmarnock proved too strong the Ayrshire club picked up its first Scottish Cup with a 3–2 victory.

However, just to prove that their Cup efforts that season had been no fluke, Albion Rovers reached the semi-finals again the following season, where, once more, Rangers were the opponents. This time round though, the Light Blues made no mistake, winning 4–1 before a crowd of 65,000 at Celtic Park.

A violent night in Glasgow, 1963

Considering the reputation for violence which has unfortunately – and perhaps unfairly – been associated with Glasgow through the years, a violent night in the city may have passed unnoticed. But this one involved an international football match and made the news headlines all round the world.

On 8 May 1963, Austria came to Hampden for the tenth meeting between the two countries, Scotland having only one victory thus far. The visitors should have felt very confident about the outcome but in truth they were very apprehensive.

On the Monday evening prior to the game they had been taken to see Rangers play Airdrie in a league game, a match characterised by some tough tackling. The Austrian players were rather surprised by the nature of some of these challenges; and they were appalled at the way the referee allowed the goalkeeper to be charged. It was no surprise then that the visiting side was edgy and tense when it came out on to the park . . . and ready to retaliate!

The Scottish team that night was Brown (Spurs), Hamilton (Dundee), Holt (Hearts), McKay (Spurs), Ure (Dundee), Baxter (Rangers), Henderson (Rangers), Gibson (Leicester), Miller (Rangers), Law (Manchester United) and Wilson (Rangers).

Scotland went quickly into a two-goal lead thanks to Davie Wilson, then the violence erupted. Centre-forward Nemec was cautioned for a bad foul; within minutes he was sent off for spitting at the referee, although he took several minutes to leave the field. Twenty minutes from the end, by which time Scotland were four-up, thanks to two further goals by Denis Law, inside-forward Hof was ordered off for a foul on Willie Henderson.

He also delayed his departure, the referee eventually bringing on police officers, not only to escort Hof from the field but also to placate the Austrian officials! Five minutes later, the match was re-started but by that time the atmosphere was very unpleasant and within minutes it once again boiled over. Outside-right Linhart fouled Law, the Scot retaliated but referee Jim Finney of England had had enough, blew his whistle and walked up the tunnel!

It was not a popular decision and an angry crowd gathered outside the entrance demanding their money back. Other fans were annoyed that the sudden decision had deprived Scotland of a fine victory.

That particular Wednesday was a sporting extravaganza. England drew with Brazil at Wembly before a crowd of 100,000; Brian London outpointed American Don Warner in Blackpool; while in Lisbon, Benfica beat Feyenoord to reach the European Cup final, where they would meet AC Milan, conquerors of Dundee in the other semi-final. Yet all over Europe, the incidents at Hampden grabbed the headlines, putting the names of Scotland and Austria on the map for all the wrong reasons.

However, for the 95,000 present that night, there was at least the satisfaction of being present at one of the most unusual and memorable nights in Scottish football.

An English referee is brought in, 1905

At the end of season 1904–05, two teams, Celtic and Rangers, were locked together at the head of the First Division table:

	P	W	D	L	F	A	Pts
Celtic	26	18	5	3	68	31	41
Rangers	26	19	3	4	83	28	41

At the time, neither goal scoring, goal average or goal difference was an accepted method of deciding the issue, a fact very much to Celtic's benefit as Rangers goal record was much the better.

The deciding method in use then was a play-off, held at Hampden Park on 6 May 1905. There had been on-field trouble that season – and the year before – in several Old Firm matches, so the SFA decided to take no chances and sent for an English referee – Mr Kirkham from Preston – to handle the tie, which Celtic won 2–1.

Bad days for the national team

In successive matches in the 2003–04 season, Scotland's national football team lost ten goals. A 0–6 loss to Holland in a European Championship play-off match in Amsterdam was followed by our biggest-ever defeat by Wales, 0–4 in a friendly at Cardiff.

Biggest wins by Scottish teams, 1881–2002

Aberdeen	13–0	v Peterhead	Scottish Cup	9.2.1923
Airdrie Utd	5–1	v Brechin	Division 2	23.11.2002
Albion Rovers	12–0	v Airdriehill	Scottish Cup	3.9.1887
Alloa Athletic	9–2	v Forfar	Division 2	18.3.1933
Arbroath	36–0	v Bon Accord	Scottish Cup	12.9.1885
Ayr United	11–1	v Dumbarton	League Cup	13.8.1952
Berwick Rangers	8–1	v Forfar	Division 2	25.12.1965
		v Vale of Leithen	Scottish Cup	17.12.1966
Brechin City	12–1	v Thornhill	Scottish Cup	28.1.1926
Celtic	11–0	v Dundee	Division 1	26.10.1895
Clyde	11–1	v Cowdenbeath	Division 2	6.10.1951
Cowdenbeath	12–0	v Johnstone	Scottish Cup	21.1.1928
Dumbarton	13–1	v Kirkintilloch	Scottish Cup	1.9.1888
Dundee	10–0	v Alloa	Division	2 9.3.1947
		v Dunfermline	Division 2	22.3.1047
Dundee United	14–0	v Nithsdale W.	Scottish Cup	17.1.1931
Dunfermline	11–2	v Stenhousemuir	Division 2	27.9.1930
East Fife	13–2	v Edinburgh City	Division 2	11.12.1937
East Stirlingshire	11–2	v Vale of Bannock	Scottish Cup	22.9.1888
Elgin City	18–1	v Brora Rangers	NOS Cup	6.2.1960
Falkirk	12–1	v Laurieston	Scottish Cup	23.9.1893
Forfar Athletic	14–1	v Lindertis	Scottish Cup	1.9.1888
Gretna	20–0	v Silloth	C & D League	1962
Greenock Morton	11–0	v Carfin Shamrock	Scottish Cup	12.11.1886
Hamilton Acad.	11–1	v Chryston	Lanarkshire Cup	28.11.1885
Heart of Midlothian	21–0	v Anchor	EFA Cup	30.10.1880
Hibernian	22–1	v 42nd Highlanders	Scottish Cup	3.9.1881
Inverness Caley T.	8–1	v Annan Athletic	Scottish Cup	24.1.1988
Kilmarnock	11–1	v Paisley Acad.	Scottish Cup	18.1.1930
Livingston	7–0	v Queen o/t South	Scottish Cup	29.1.2000
Montrose	12–0	v Vale of Leithen	Scottish Cup	13.11.1886
Motherwell	12–1	v Dundee United	Division 2	23.1.1954
Partick Thistle	16–0	v Royal Albert	Scottish Cup	17.1.1931

Peterhead	17–0	v Fort William	Highland League	1998/99
Queen o/t South	11–1	v Stranraer	Scottish Cup	16.1.1932
Queen's Park	16–0	v St Peter's	Scottish Cup	29.8.1885
Raith Rovers	10–1	v Coldstream	Scottish Cup	13.2.1954
Rangers	14–2	v Blairgowrie	Scottish Cup	20.1.1934
Ross County	11–0	v St Cuthbert Wand.	Scottish Cup	Dec. 1933
St Johnstone	9–0	v Albion Rovers	League Cup	9.3.1946
St Mirren	15–0	v Glasgow Univ.	Scottish Cup	30.1.1960
Stenhousemuir	9–2	v Dundee United	Division 2	19.4.1937
Stirling Albion	20–0	v Selkirk	Scottish Cup	8.12.1984
Stranraer	7–0	v Brechin City	Division 2	6.2.1965

20 or more goals scored: Arbroath, Hearts, Hibs, Stirling Albion, Gretna
SPL teams mentioned in losing columns: Dundee United (2), Dundee
Highest winning score: 36–0 Arbroath
Smallest winning margin: 5–1 Airdrie

Biggest attendance

The biggest attendance for a league match in Scotland is the 118,567 who gathered at Ibrox on 2 January 1938 for the Old Firm league encounter.

Brits among the foreign visitors

When the Scottish League played their Italian counterparts at Hampden in November 1961, the match ended in a 1–1 draw.

Eight of the visitors were Italian. The other three were Gerry Hitchens (England), John Charles (Wales) and Scotland's own Denis Law.

Close to you!

The two clubs situated closest to each other geographically in British football are Dundee and Dundee United, both of which are on the same street, Tannadice Street, about 100 yards apart.

However, they are not the closest in Europe. The home ground of MTK-VM Budapest abuts that of BKV Elore, making them the closest neighbours in world football.

Death of a young legend

A young Fifer called John Thomson made his debut in goal for Celtic against Dundee at Dens Park on 12 February 1927. He had just turned

18 at the time but quickly made a name for himself, becoming a regular for both the Parkhead club and his country.

One month after Thomson picked up his second medal as Celtic beat Motherwell 4–2 in the replay of the 1931 Scottish Cup final, a party of players, management and directors left on tour for North America. It was a successful trip, the club playing 13 games, of which 9 were won, 3 lost and 1 drawn, with 48 goals for and 18 against.

While Celtic were in North America, Rangers signed a very promising and prolific centre-forward from Yoker Athletic, Sam English. He soon made the first team and showed up well, recovering from a slight injury to take the field for his first Old Firm match at Ibrox on 5 September 1931.

The crowd was large on a fine sultry afternoon – 75,000 – but the play was nervous, with many errors creeping in. Five minutes after the interval, with the game still goalless, Ranger's right-winger Fleming pushed the ball in front of Sam English and he raced towards the goal. Just as he prepared to shoot, Johnny Thomson ran out from the Celtic goal and dived to block the shot. English rose limping; Thomson lay where he fell.

Trainer, manager and doctor raced on to the field; a stretcher was called for. The incident occurred at the Rangers end and their support, like fans everywhere, were not unhappy to see an opponent go down. A section even cheered. However, Rangers captain Davie Meiklejohn was quick to go behind the goal and gesture for silence; it was an effective appeal and Thomson was stretchered off in peace and quiet. Chic Geatons went into goal for Celtic but the heart had gone out of play and it petered out into a goalless draw.

Some six hours later, Johnny Thomson died from his injuries in the Victoria Infirmary. He was twenty-three years old.

Did you like it? Scotland's World Cup anthem, 1982

In 1982 the Scottish World Cup Squad put out their record, 'We have a dream'. Unfortunately the team did not reach the later stages of the

World Cup, but the record is ranked fifth in the list of top-ten singles in the United Kingdom by sports stars.

Down to 7: when Scots were mistaken for Englishmen

After winning the European Cup in Lisbon in 1967, Celtic earned the right to challenge the champions of South America for the World Club Championship.

There had been seven of these matches up to that point, with Europe winning three (Real Madrid 1960; Inter-Milan 1964 & 1965) and South America four (Penarol 1961 & 1966; Santos 1962 & 1963).

Eventually, Racing Club of Buenos Aires won the right to play the European champions and the first leg was pencilled in for 18 October 1967. In order to accommodate the huge crowd expected for such an important game, the Celtic officials switched the venue from Parkhead to Hampden where, on a cold night, 90,000 turned up.

And they were not disappointed with what they saw. Celtic played well on the night and a single goal by Billy McNeill gave the Scots club victory. However, the game was punctuated by frequent displays by the South Americans of the dark arts of the game. Blatant body-checking, spitting, jersey- and hair-pulling and violent tackles were the norm, the Spanish referee doing his best to quell such dubious challenges.

Two weeks later, the teams came out for the second leg before a crowd of 120,000 in the Mozart Y Cuyo, Avellaneda in Buenos Aires. It was a veritable cauldron of hate although, by that time, as one of the players involved, I knew the reason why.

The previous year, in the World Cup tournament, England had met Argentina in the quarter-final stage at Wembley. It turned out to be a rough match, with the South American side eventually losing its captain, Rattin, and England winning 1–0.

In discussing the play in an interview later that evening, the English manager, Alf Ramsay, eschewing his normal caution and civility, made his contempt for the Argentinians clear, describing them as 'animals'. His words reverberated throughout the football world, no more so than in

South America, where countries not normally associated with friendly feelings towards each other united in condemning him and vowed to settle matters at some future date.

Unfortunately, that meant the matches against Celtic. Everyone we met seemed to be totally unaware of the difference between Scotland and England; we were joined together under the same monarchy and government, therefore we must be the same. So, we would be the whipping boys on whom to vent their anger and frustration. The first leg at Hampden gave us all a taste of what we might expect in South America; unfortunately, the reality was even worse.

Before the match even started, goalkeeper Ronnie Simpson was hit by some form of missile from the crowd and had to be replaced by John Fallon. Once begun, the play was broken up by similar challenges to those seen at Hampden, only of a more blatant nature and more frequently. The Celtic players found it difficult to maintain their normal rhythm in the midst of such mayhem. Racing won the game 2–1 and in the absence of the away goals rule at that time (which would have resulted in Celtic winning) a third match was required.

The Celtic party was split over competing further against opponents who were determined to win by any means. Some tough talking went on behind the scenes, the decision to play apparently being led by Jock Stein, with the Celtic chairman, Sir Robert Kelly, very much in favour of heading home.

Stein seemed to win out, we travelled across the River Plate by plane and, in front of a crowd of 75,000 in the Centenario Stadium, Montevideo, ran out to face Racing Club for the third time in 18 days, the contest under the control of Señor Osorio of Paraguay.

From the start, the referee did not have control of the match. Initially, he allowed the Argentinians too much leeway in their roughhouse tactics, and this time many Celtic players lost their tempers. Six players were dismissed in total, four of them Celts (Lennox, Johnstone, Hughes and Auld, although the latter refused to leave the field and stayed on for the whole match); police were twice brought on to the pitch to restore order, and centre-forward Cardenas scored the only goal of the game.

It was not one of the better days in Celtic's history and the image of the club suffered. Although the management and directorate had taken the debatable decision to play the third game, that seemed to be forgotten as the players received the brunt of the blame, all participants being fined £250 for their part in the proceedings.

That the event should be included in a book like this can be easily explained. Firstly, it remains a unique occasion, the only time a Scots club has competed in that championship. Secondly, seldom in the history of Scottish football has a team had four players sent off, far less a team competing in the final of the World Club Championship. Thirdly, I should imagine that a Scottish club side has never played in front of almost 290,000 spectators in the space of 18 days.

And lastly, if that same competition had taken place three years later, with the away goals rule in place, Celtic would have been acclaimed World Club Champions.

Dons lead the way

The first ground in Britain to have a dugout was Pittodrie Stadium, in Aberdeen.

The club's trainer in the 1920s – Donald Coleman – believed he could learn more about his players' movements through watching their feet at ground level. He needed dry conditions in which to note his observations so the club installed a dugout for that purpose.

Aberdeen FC also led the way in another field in 1978, when the directors decided that the ground should be all-seated. Pittodrie became the first in Britain to do so, followed shortly afterwards by Clydebank's Kilbowie Park.

European Trophy Winners, 1972–83

In season 1971–72, under the leadership of Willie Waddell, Rangers became the first Scottish team to win the European Cup-Winner's Cup, having had to overcome some tough opposition along the way.

In round one, they beat Rennes 2–1; in round two, they had a tougher job against Sporting Lisbon, going through on the away goals rule after the teams finished locked 6–6 (see p. 54). In the quarter-final, Torino proved equally difficult, Rangers winning 2–1, while old rivals Bayern Munich were overcome in the semi-final by 3–1.

Unfortunately, after-match trouble at the final in Barcelona has tended to deflect from Ranger's triumph but they did play really well to beat Dynamo Moscow 3–2 and take the trophy back to Ibrox – and Scotland – for the first time.

Team: McCloy, Jardine, Johnstone, Smith, Mathieson, Greig, Conn, McDonald, McLean, Stein, Johnston.

In the 1982–83 season, Aberdeen became only the third Scottish side to win in Europe when they also won the European Cup-Winner's Cup. The Dons had a comfortable 11–1 start in the preliminary round against FC Sion.

In the first round proper, though, only a single goal took them through against Dynamo Tirana. Round two was easier, 3–0 against Lech Poznan; then a fine 3–2 away victory over Bayern Munich in the quarters took them through to the semi-finals, where they beat Waterschei 5–1. For the final against Real Madrid in Gothenburg, manager Alex Ferguson drilled his team well and they rose to the occasion, although needing extra-time to dispose of the Spanish stars by two goals to one.

Team: Leighton, Rougvie, McLeish, Miller, MacMaster, Cooper, Strachan, Simpson, McGhee, Black (Hewitt), Weir.

Fifers on the way: East Fife, 1938

At the end of Season 1936–37 there was the biggest ever attendance at a Scottish Cup final at Hampden Park when Aberdeen were beaten 2–1 by Celtic in front of a crowd 147,365. In their run to that season's final Celtic had beaten East Fife 3–0 in the first round. East Fife were a good side at the time; they had quality players. But teams from outside the big names seldom go far in any competition. Yet in the Cup of 1937–38, East Fife went on all the way, becoming the first Second Division team to win the trophy.

Round	Date	Opposition	Score	Attendance
1	22.1.38	Airdrie	1–2	5,000
2	12.2.38	Dundee Utd (H)	5–0	11,000
3	5.3.38	Aberdeen (H)	1–1	17,000
Replay	9.3.38	Aberdeen (A)	1–2	25,499
4	19.3.38	Raith Rovers (H)	2–2	19,000
Replay	23.3.38	Raith Rovers (A)	3–2	25,490
5	2.4.38	St Bernard's (Tynecastle)	1–1	34,000
Replay	6.4.38	St Bernard's (Tynecastle)	1–1	30,185
2nd Replay	13.4.38	St Bernard's	2–1	32,564
Final	23.4.38	Kilmarnock (Hampden)	1–1	80,091 92,716
Replay	27.4.38	Kilmarnock (Hampden)	4–2	

First in Europe: Hibs, 1950s

Hibs were Britain's first representatives in European football when they entered the European Cup in season 1955–56.

In their opening tie, they beat Rot-Weiss Essen of Germany 5–1 on aggregate. Both legs of their quarter-final tie against Djugardens of Sweden were played in Scotland due to adverse weather conditions in Scandinavia, the 'away' leg at Firhill Stadium, the ground of Partick Thistle. Hibs won 1–0 at Easter Road and 3–1 'away'.

In the semi-finals, the Edinburgh club found Stade de Reims of France a little too strong, losing 0–2 away and 0–1 at home.

First Scotland v England fooball

In the late autumn of 1870, the Secretary of the Football Association, C.W. Alcock, wrote to some Scottish newspapers indicating that the FA intended to select teams of English and Scottish players to compete against each other at the Oval on 19 November 1870.

He invited nominations, stating rather arrogantly: 'In Scotland, once essentially the land of football, there should still be a spark left of the old fire and I confidently appeal to Scotsmen ...' As he no doubt expected, the Scots could not resist the challenge, but the team which ran out consisted mainly of expatriate Scots living in London, or friends of those with rather tenuous Scottish connections.

Four of these matches were played, all at the same venue, in 1870 and 1871, their success encouraging the organisers to arrange an official contest. The rugby men, however, were quicker on the draw and the first-ever Scotland–England encounter (excluding Bannockburn, Flodden etc.) was held at Raeburn Place, Edinburgh in 1871. This match was won by Scotland by a goal and one try, watched by a crowd estimated at between 2,000 and 4,000.

Just over a year later the first official Scotland v England football match was played at Hamilton Crescent, in the west of Glasgow, on 30th November 1872, the game starting at 2 p.m. Admission was 1 shilling, and about 2,000 turned up to see the action, paying £109 in total at the gate.

The Scots, all from Queen's Park, were smaller and lighter than their opponents but used their teamwork to control the game, managing to stop the inspired dribbling of the English forwards.

The match ended in a 0–0 draw, a result repeated only twice in these matches ever since, in 1970 and 1987.

Floodlights: Stenhousemuir, 1870s–1950s

There were innovations in the early days at various grounds as regards floodlights, but some accidents occurred, as at Kilmarnock in 1878 when two players were so badly injured after three lights failed that they had to retire permanently from the game.

One of the first experiments in Scotland took place at Celtic Park, when, on Christmas Day 1893, a friendly was played under artificial lighting against Clyde. A crowd of 5,000 people turned up on a wintry night to see the match, which was played under lighting supplied by sixteen arc lights suspended from wires stretched across the field. Unfortunately, some stoppages in play were unavoidable when the ball struck the wires, so the idea was abandoned until a later date.

That later date in Scottish football came in 1951, the occasion a floodlit friendly at Ochilview Park between local team, Stenhousemuir

(The Warriors), and Hibs. The term 'floodlighting' must here be used with qualification. The lights that shone down that evening were little stronger than bright street-lamps and were well below the standard that we would regard as normal today. However, at a time when Britain was still recovering from the problems of the Second World War, it was a remarkable and very far-sighted step for such a club to take.

Football: the 1950s

The 1950s was an amazing time for Scottish Football. Compared to other eras, the number of teams which won one of the three major Scottish trophies was quite astonishing.

Let's first of all show the years immediately after the Second World War:

	League	*Scottish Cup*	*League Cup*
1946–47	Rangers	Aberdeen	Rangers
1947–48	Hibs	Rangers	East Fife
1948–49	Rangers	Rangers	Rangers
1949–50	Rangers	Rangers	East Fife

A total of 5 winning teams in 12 competitions.

If we then list the winners for the early 1960s:

	League	*Scottish Cup*	*League Cup*
1960–61	Rangers	Dunfermline	Rangers
1961–62	Dundee	Rangers	Rangers
1962–63	Rangers	Rangers	Hearts
1963–64	Rangers	Rangers	Rangers

A total of 4 winning teams in 12 competitions.

If we then show the list for the decade of the 1950s, quite a different picture emerges:

	League	*Scottish Cup*	*League Cup*
1950–51	Hibs	Celtic	Motherwell
1951–52	Hibs	Motherwell	Dundee
1952–53	Rangers	Rangers	Dundee
1953–54	Celtic	Celtic	East Fife
1954–55	Aberdeen	Clyde	Hearts
1955–56	Rangers	Hearts	Aberdeen

	League	Scottish Cup	League Cup
1956–57	Rangers	Falkirk	Celtic
1957–58	Hearts	Clyde	Celtic
1958–59	Rangers	St Mirren	Hearts
1959–60	Hearts	Rangers	Hearts

A total of 11 different teams in 30 competitions.

Truly, the 1950s was the most fascinating decade of the 20th century for Scottish football.

Football and quoits: Willie Cringan, 1910–26

Willie Cringan was a professional footballer from 1910 to 1925, his career extending through Sunderland, Celtic, the RAF, Third Lanark, Motherwell and Inverness Thistle. He even later became coach to Belgium in 1952.

However, he did not neglect his other sporting talents and became Scottish Quoits Champion in September 1926.

Football – and rugby: Henry Waugh Renny-Tailyour, 1849–1920

Henry Waugh Renny-Tailyour was born in Mussoorie, North West Provinces, India on 9 October 1849. He came back to Britain ten years later and was educated at Cheltenham College, where he possibly played soccer. In 1868 he entered the Royal Military Academy, and was commissioned in 1870. Much of his spare time was spent in sports activities, both soccer and rugger.

His football career was spent with the Royal Engineers. Renny-Tailyour was a member of the RE sides which won runner-up positions in the FA Cup in 1872 and 1874: in 1875, they went one better, beating Old Etonians 2–0 at the Oval after a 1–1 draw.

Two years before that, in Scotland's second international football match, like the first against England, although this time in London, Renny-Tailyour was at outside right as the Scots went down 2–4. He did, however, score the first goal.

Quite amazingly, in the course of this football career, Renny-Tailyour managed to fit in a rugby cap. The FA Cup final appearance in 1872 mentioned above occurred on 16 March, when the Royal Engineers side lost 1–0 to Wanderers at the Oval.

Just over a month earlier, on 5 February 1872, at the same venue, Renny-Tailyour was in the forwards of the 20–man team when Scotland played its second rugby international, losing to England by a goal. Although 4,000 spectators turned up to see this clash, only 2,000 watched the FA Cup final the following month.

Following his retirement from the army in 1889, Renny-Tailyour became assistant managing director of Guinness. Between 1913 and 1919, he was the company's managing director. He was also a fine cricketer, playing for the Royal Engineers, Kent between 1873 and 1883, and Aberdeenshire occasionally; he also turned out three times for the Gentlemen against the Players.

Henry Waugh Renny-Tailyour died on 15 June 1920 and remains the only Scot to have represented his country at both association football and rugby.

Footballer father – singer son

When Celtic Football Club toured the USA in 1951, they were recommended to have a look at a Jamaican star playing for a team in Detroit.

Gil Heron came to Scotland in July of that year, scored twice in the club's public trial in August, and went on to play five games for the first team in the early part of the season.

The following year he departed for Third Lanark and Kidderminster Harriers; but not before playing some cricket for Poloc and Ferguslie. Gil eventually returned to Detroit, where he published two books of poetry and fathered a son, who later found fame – under the name Gil Scott-Heron – as a jazz legend.

Goal scoring in various ways, 1885–1979

Throughout the history of football, there have been many occasions when the goal-scoring feats of one player have earned him the term of 'man of the match'. We can go as far back as 1885, for instance, to recall the 13 goals scored by John Petrie when Arbroath beat Bon Accord 36–0 in a Scottish Cup first-round tie – both Scottish records to this day.

In 1904, Jimmy Quinn of Celtic became the first professional player to score a hat-trick in the Scottish Cup final, a feat emulated only by Dixie Deans of Celtic, in 1972, and Gordon Durie of Rangers in 1996. The first player to score a final hat-trick was J. Smith of Queens Park in the 3–1 win over Dumbarton in 1881.

Only one player has ever scored five goals for the Scottish national side, Hughie Gallacher against Northern Ireland in 1929, although Denis Law, with four against both Northern Ireland (1962) and Norway (1963), as well as Colin Stein's four against Cyprus (1969), ran him close.

Surely one of the oddest occurrences in the goal-scoring stakes came in the League Cup final of 1974 when Joe Harper of Hibs notched a hat-trick yet his team was on the receiving end of 6–3 defeat by Celtic, for whom Dixie Deans also scored three. The League Cup-final record, in fact, is held by Jim Forrest, of Rangers, who scored four against Morton in 1963.

But goal-scoring exploits can occur in unusual circumstances. The evening of 3 December, 1977, was clear and crisp and the pitch at Hampden was rather hard for the Second Division match between Queen's Park and East Stirling. Halfway through the first-half, Queen's Park were awarded a corner and centre half Alan Mackin trotted up to make use of his 6 ft 2 in height. The kicker signalled a high cross to the near post, but lost his footing as he struck the ball, which bobbled to the near post. Mackin raced in, expecting the high cross, slowed down to meet the ball, stumbled as he did so and the ball struck his knee before sliding into the net.

Mackin returned to his position rather embarrassed to receive the congratulations. East Stirling then kicked off to restart the match; the ball was played to the right winger, who raced down the line before hammering a low cross along the six-yard box. Before any of his team-mates could reach it, in stepped Mackin to deal with the situation. To his horror he sent a volley into the roof of the net for the equaliser. He thus entered the record books for scoring a goal and an own goal within 45 seconds.

Two years later, on 8 December 1979, Neil Hood of Clyde also had a day to remember. Playing against Airdrie in a First Division match, Hood scored both the Clyde goals, gave away the penalty which led to Airdrie's only reply, and then was ordered off shortly before the end. Just to add insult to injury, a radio reporter announced later that it had not been much of a game.

Hearts show the way, 1915–2003

In the history of the First Division Championship (or the Premier Division or the Premier League) only five teams have scored a hundred or more goals in a single season:

Season	Team	Matches	Goals
1915–16	Celtic	38	116
1919–20	Rangers	42	106
1927–28	Rangers	38	109
1928–29	Rangers	38	109
1931–32	Motherwell	38	119
	Rangers	38	118
1932–33	Rangers	38	113
Season	Team	Matches	Goals
1933–34	Rangers	38	114
1935–36	Celtic	38	115
1937–38	Celtic	38	114
1938–39	Rangers	38	112
1957–58	Hearts	34	132
1959–60	Hearts	34	102
1965–66	Celtic	34	106
1966–67	Celtic	34	111
1967–68	Celtic	34	106
1991–92	Rangers	44	101
2002–03	Rangers	38	101
2003–04	Celtic	38	105

The Hearts' statistics for 1957–58 are quite astonishing. One of the most difficult arts in football is to score goals at one end without losing too many at the other. In that season, while Hearts were scoring an average of 3.8 goals per game, they lost only 29 in total.

Ibrox disaster 1902

In the early days of Scottish football the rivalry between Celtic and Rangers was not confined to the game itself. The competition to have the best stadium was also intense.

Ibrox had been chosen to host the lucrative Scotland–England fixture of 1892 but the new Celtic Park got the preference in 1894, 1896, 1898 and 1900. Ibrox, of course, was then restructured (in 1899) and was again awarded the 1902 contest.

Tragically, as the crowd of 68,114 were gathered in the stadium watching the early moments of play, the wooden terracing in one rear section 'collapsed like a trap door'. A 25-yard square void quickly appeared, sending 125 spectators tumbling 50 feet through the framework to the ground below. Many were saved because they landed on the bodies of those below, but in all 26 were killed and 500 injured. Yet most of the crowd were quite unaware of what had occurred, and the players only found out about the tragedy at the interval. Even so, it was decided that the game should go on to avoid an even worse scene, and the play ended in a 1–1 draw. However, it was immediately declared an unofficial international and the two countries met again a month later at Birmingham, where the match finished 2–2.

Ibrox disaster 1971

Around 80,000 packed into Ibrox on 2 January 1971 for the second Old Firm league clash of the 1970–1971 season.

In the table, Celtic were 8 points ahead of Rangers, with 18 games played, but the match was still the subject of much contemplation and discussion by both sets of fans, keen to put one over on their major rivals. The play was as frantic as ever in these contests but neither side gave any quarter and with 2 minutes left the score was still 0–0. Then a shot by Bobby Lennox from 25 yards rebounded off the cross bar and Jimmy

Johnstone pounced to prod the ball home. The Celtic fans roared their appreciation: at the other end, hundreds of Rangers fans headed for the exit in disappointment.

However, with only seconds left, Rangers were awarded a free-kick out on the left. Davie Smith floated a cross into the middle of the Celtic defence and Colin Stein appeared from nowhere to grab the equaliser. A simple goal, a deserved equaliser, yet it precipitated the second Ibrox Disaster.

Those who had started to leave heard the roar of acclamation from the Rangers support and tried to come back up the stairs, hoping to share in the celebrations. Unfortunately, they were confronted by a wall of fans coming down the stairs and a crush developed. Most of the horror occurred at stairway 13, where the crowd collapsed 'as though into a hole in the ground' as onlookers described it.

At the end of the most tragic day in Scottish football, 66 fans lay dead and many more were seriously injured.

It happened at Hampden

1904: 64,472 Scottish Cup Final – First final at third Hampden Park

1906: 102,741 Scotland v England – First six-figure attendance for any game in Scotland

1908: 121,452 Scotland v England – World-record gate at that time

1912: 127,307 Scotland v England – World-record gate at that time

1925: 101,714 Celtic v Rangers Scottish Cup SF – First six-figure crowd for a club game in Scotland

1928: 118,115 Celtic v Rangers Scottish Cup Final – Record crowd for a club match in Scotland

1930: 95,772 Queen's Park v Rangers – World-record gate for a match involving an amateur club

1931: 129,810 Scotland v England – World-record gate at the time

1933: 136,259 Scotland v England – World-record gate at the time

1937: 147,365 Celtic v Aberdeen Scottish Cup Final – World-record crowd for a national cup final; still the biggest attendance for a club match in Europe

1937: 147,415 Scotland v England – All-time record for a European international match

1944: 133,000 Scotland v England – Record wartime gate in Great Britain

1946: 139,468 Scotland v England – Record gate for an unofficial international

1948: 143,570 Rangers v Hibs Scottish Cup SF – Record attendance for a non-final game

1948: 129,176 & 133,570 Rangers v Morton Scottish Cup Final and replay – Largest combined crowd for a final plus replay

1954: 113,056 Scotland v Hungary – Biggest crowd ever for a match involving Hungary

1960: 127,621 Real Madrid v Eintracht Frankfurt European Cup Final – Record gate for a European Cup Final

1963: 105,907 Rangers v Morton League Cup Final – First six-figure crowd for a League Cup Final

1965: 107,609 Celtic v Rangers League Cup Final – All-time record gate for a British League Cup Final

1970: 136,505 Celtic v Leeds United European Cup SF – All time record for a European Cup game

Jimmy Delaney

Jimmy Delaney was an extremely talented outside-right who made headlines throughout his career.

He joined Celtic in 1933 and made his first team debut in August 1934, quickly becoming a first-team regular and earning a place in the national team.

Delaney was at outside-right when Scotland beat England 3–1 at Hampden on 17 April 1937 before an attendance of 149,547. One week later he played in the Scottish Cup Final for Celtic against Aberdeen at the same venue, where 147,365 were present. So, over the space of two matches in one week, Jimmy Delaney played in front of almost 300,000 spectators!

He also played for Celtic when they won the Empire Exhibition Trophy in 1938, suffered such a badly-fractured arm against Aberdeen on 1 April 1939 that surgeons wanted to amputate, but made his comeback on 2 August 1941.

In 1946 Delaney left for Manchester United, with whom he won an FA Cup winner's medal in 1948, moved via Aberdeen and Falkirk to

Derry City, where he won an Irish Cup medal in 1954, and just missed out on another the following season, when, as player-manager of Cork Athletic, he only managed a runners-up medal in Eire.

Lisbon

When Jock Stein took over as Celtic Manager in March 1965, the Glasgow club had not won the League Cup in eight years nor the League Championship or the Scottish Cup either for eleven years.

Two years later, his reorganised side flew to Lisbon to meet Inter Milan in the final of the European Cup. Quite a transformation!

In the campaign that year, Celtic had beaten Zurich 5–0 over two legs in round one and Nantes 6–2 in the second round. The quarter-final stage proved more difficult, Celtic scoring only in the final minute of the home leg to record a 2–1 victory over Vojvodina Novisad: while Dukla Prague were put to the sword in the semi-final, a fine 3–1 win at Celtic Park followed by a forgettable 0–0 draw in Czechoslovakia. Still, the end justified the means.

As the team came out for the 1967 European Cup final in Lisbon, 55,000 fans were packed into the Estadio Nacional, many from Scotland and a fair percentage making their first trip abroad.

Celtic went one-down to a Mazzola penalty in only seven minutes but immediately took control of the match, only superb goalkeeping by Sarti keeping them at bay. Even he was powerless though, to stop the shots by Gemmell (63) and Chalmers (85) which gave Celtic the trophy.

Several records were broken that day. Celtic became the first side from a non-Latin country to win the Cup; and the first British side to do so. Even more incredibly, the eleven players who represented Celtic in that final were all Scots – born within thirty miles of Celtic Park.

Team: Ronnie Simpson, Glasgow; Jim Craig, Glasgow; Tommy Gemmell, Craigneuk, Lanarkshire; Bobby Murdoch, Bothwell, Lanarkshire; Billy McNeill, Bellshill, Lanarkshire; John Clark, Bellshill; Jimmy Johnstone, Viewpark, Lanarkshire; Willie Wallace, Kirkintilloch, Dunbartonshire; Steve Chalmers, Glasgow; Bertie Auld, Glasgow; Bobby Lennox, Saltcoats, Ayrshire.

Names on the Scottish Cup, 1874–92

A total of 23 teams have won the Scottish Cup, but only 8 teams, who won between 1874 and 1892, have actually had their names etched on the trophy. These are Queens Park, Vale of Leven, Dumbarton, Renton, Hibs, Third Lanark, Hearts and Celtic. The names of all the other winners are inscribed on the base.

Nicknames

Only a very memorable team or a group of players are given nicknames but when they are given these they tend to be used through the decades. For instance:

The Lisbon Lions were the eleven players whose attacking and inspirational football made Celtic the first British club to lift the European Cup when, on 25 May 1967, they defeated Internazionale of Milan 2–1 in the final of that year's tournament at the national stadium in Lisbon. Their story is told elsewhere in this book.

In the early 1950s Hibs had a very famous forward line that got the name of the Famous Five from a series of books by the author Enid Blyton. The Hibs Famous Fives' exploits included winning the Scottish League title in 1948, 1951 and 1952. The team had Gordon Smith at outside right, an elegant Scottish winger who did not play for either of the Old Firm but is the only Scot to have competed in the European Cup for three different Scottish Clubs: Dundee, Heart of Midlothian and Hibernian. At inside right was the tricky and skilful Bobby Johnstone. At centre forward was Laurie Reilly, regarded by many observers as the finest centre forward in Britain at that time. Eddie Turnbull provided flair and power at inside left; and at outside left was the speedy Willie Ormond who later became the manager of Scotland and took them to the 1974 World Cup Finals. Eddie Turnbull later became Hibernian Manager himself and created another exciting Hibs team in the early 1970s that were themselves nicknamed 'Turnbull's Tornadoes'.

Heart of Midlothian, Hibs' great rivals in Edinburgh, were noted for their inside forward trio in the 1950s, nicknamed the 'Terrible Trio'.

This featured Alfie Conn at inside right, Willie Bauld at centre forward and Jimmy Wardhaugh at inside left. These three spearheaded the prolific Hearts attack as they took the 1956 Scottish Cup, the 1958 League title and the League Cup in 1954 and 1958.

Conn's son, also Alfie, won a League title and a Scottish Cup medal with Celtic and a Scottish Cup medal with Rangers, both in the 1970s.

And speaking of the Light Blues from Glasgow, in the late 1940s their team had such an impressive defence that it came to be known as 'the Iron Curtain'. And that comprised Bobby Brown in goal; fullbacks George Young and Jock Shaw; and half-backs Ian McColl, Willie Woodburn and Sammy Cox.

Off to war: Hearts and Celtic, 1914–18

Rather surprisingly, the outbreak of the Great War in 1914 was greeted by scenes of enthusiasm.

All over Europe, crowds gathered to cheer the men going to the front. In Russia, Austria, France and Germany, the soldiers were fêted and presented with flowers or even kissed and cuddled by grateful women. Everyone was quite happy to be going, as they all thought it would not last long and that their side would win.

Britain's army was small compared to other nations, even when the Territorials and reservists were added. So, when war broke out a call was made for 100,000 volunteers to sign up. In the event, almost half a million came forward to answer the call!

By November of that first year it was becoming clear that the war would not be over soon. The reality of the conflict began to hit home, as the wounded began to return and many others felt obliged to join the forces as part of their duty. Among these were footballers playing in Scotland.

Those wearing the maroon of Hearts, for instance, had a particular dilemma. For the first time since 1897 the club had a chance of winning a league title, but many folk were wondering about the importance of football when your fellow countrymen were dying on the other side of the Channel. The Hearts stars obviously felt that they had a duty to their country, as the entire first-team squad enlisted at the end of November. They were giving up around four pounds per week to earn the soldier's pay of eight shillings and twopence (42p) a week!

Tragically, seven did not survive: Private James Speedie, died Loos, 1915, aged 21; Corporal Tom Gracie, died Glasgow, 1915, aged 26; Private Henry Wattie, died the Somme, 1915, aged 21; Private Ernest Ellis, died the Somme, 1915, aged 30; L Cpl James Boyd, died the Somme, 1915, aged 30; Sgt Duncan Currie, died the Somme, 1915, aged 23; Sgt John Allan, died Arras, 1917, aged 30.

The following survived: A.B. Ness, N. Moreland, G.P. Miller, N. Findlay, J. MacDonald, W. Scott, J. Hazeldean, J. Wilson, A. Briggs, E. McGuire, J. Low, R. Malcolm, C. Hallwood, R. Preston, H. Graham, J. Whyte, G. Sinclair, J. Frew, J. Gilbert, C. Blackhall, J. McKenzie, R. Mercer, J. Martin.

Other clubs also had their heroes. Willie Angus, who signed for Celtic in 1911 and played for the reserve side in the following two seasons, became the first Scottish Territorial soldier to win the Victoria Cross.

Angus won his VC on 12 June, at Givenchy. He lost an eye, damaged a foot and was wounded around forty times in the act of rescuing Lt James Martin, who ironically came from the same town – Carluke – as Angus.

Old Firm domination – from the 1960s

From the start of the 1960s until the present day, only four teams – on six separate occasions – have prevented a clean sweep of League Championships by the Old Firm.

In 1961–62, a very talented Dundee side finished three points clear of Rangers. A year later, the Dark Blues showed their class by reaching the semi-final of the European Cup, before losing out to AC Milan. In

1964–65 the campaign went to the last day. Kilmarnock travelled to Tynecastle knowing they needed to beat Hearts by two clear goals to take the title on goal average. This they duly did in a 2–0 win, much to the disgust of Hearts. And one could appreciate the disappointment of the Gorgie Road men. Both teams had exactly the same record (22 wins, 6 draws, 6 losses) but Hearts had scored 90 goals, conceding 49, whereas Kilmarnock had only scored 62, conceding 33. This gave Hearts a goal average of 1.837 to Kilmarnock's 1.839, so the Ayrshire team took the title (See NB below).

Under the guidance of Alex Ferguson, a very fine Aberdeen side took three titles in 1978–79, 1983–84 and 1984–85, while Jim McLean led Dundee United to their only championship in 1982–83.

Apart from these six occasions, the other League Championships since 1960 have been won by either Celtic or Rangers.

NB Hearts' bitter disappointment at losing the title in 1964–65 by goal average prompted them to propose to the Scottish League that goal difference, rather than goal average, should be used to decide such ties. The Scottish League adopted the idea and put it into effect.

Unfortunately, when Hearts were next involved in a tie for the Championship – they finished on the same points as Celtic in the season 1985–86 – they lost the title on goal difference, with a total of 26 to Celtic's 29. If goal average had still been in operation, they would have won it, with 1.783 to Celtic's 1.763.

One appearance, one touch, one goal, 1977

Against Sweden, in 1977, Celtic striker Joe Craig came on as a substitute and headed home Scotland's third goal in the 3–1 victory.

That was the one and only time he touched the ball in that game. Indeed, as Craig never received another 'cap', it proved to be his only touch in international football.

Only four sides broke the Old Firm domination , 1890–1939

Compared to the Scottish Cup, comparatively few teams have won the Scottish League.

In fact, if we take the years from its inception in 1890–91 to the cessation of football just before the Second World War, only four teams managed to break the stranglehold of the Old Firm.

Year	Champions	Year	Champions
1890–91	Dumbarton	1914–15	Celtic
	Rangers	1915–16	Celtic
1891–92	Dumbarton	1916–17	Celtic
1892–93	Celtic	1917–18	Rangers
1893–94	Celtic	1918–19	Celtic
1894–95	Hearts	1919–20	Rangers
1895–96	Celtic	1920–21	Rangers
1896–97	Hearts	1921–22	Celtic
1897–98	Celtic	1922–23	Rangers
1898–99	Rangers	1923–24	Rangers
1899–00	Rangers	1924–25	Rangers
1900–01	Rangers	1925–26	Celtic
1901–02	Rangers	1926–27	Rangers
1902–03	Hibernian	1927–28	Rangers
1903–04	Third Lanark	1928–29	Rangers
1904–05	Celtic	1929–30	Rangers
1905–06	Celtic	1930–31	Rangers
1906–07	Celtic	1931–32	Motherwell
1907–08	Celtic	1932–33	Rangers
1908–09	Celtic	1933–34	Rangers
1909–10	Celtic	1934–35	Rangers
1910–11	Rangers	1935–36	Celtic
1911–12	Rangers	1936–37	Rangers
1912–13	Rangers	1937–38	Celtic
1913–14	Celtic	1938–39	Rangers

That very talented Dumbarton side was the first, sharing the first title and winning the second outright. Hearts were next, picking up the championship twice in three years between 1894 and 1897. Hibs had a purple patch at the start of the 20th century, winning the Scottish Cup in 1902 and the league the following year.

Third Lanark won their only title in 1903–04, becoming the third Glasgow club to do so. Like Hibs, they also won the Scottish Cup around the same era, their victory coming in 1905.

Possibly the best performance of them all, however, came in 1931–32 when a Motherwell side needed to be talented and consistent to hold off the challenge of the Old Firm at the height of their powers. Not only did they win, they finished a comfortable five points ahead of their nearest rivals.

Over the ton: Kenny Dalglish, 1960–1990

The only Scottish player ever to be capped more than 100 times is Kenny Dalglish. His 102 Scottish caps is obviously a record and his 30 goals matched the tally of Denis Law.

Dalglish signed as a schoolboy for Celtic in 1968 and having secured nine major trophies, including the League and Cup double in 1972, moved to Liverpool in 1977 for a British-record fee of £440,000. His play did much to extend Liverpool's pre-eminence as the most efficient in Britain. Between 1978 and 1985 Liverpool won three European Cup finals, five League titles and four consecutive League Cup finals.

In 1985 Dalglish became player/manager and extended the run of success by guiding the club to a League and FA Cup double in 1986, plus two further League titles in 1988 and 1990. In 1991 he resigned from Liverpool but later joined Blackburn as manager and took the club to the Premiership title in 1995.

Premier Scots: the manager in England, 1990s–2000s

Since the Premiership trophy replaced the old First Division Championship in England in the 1992–93 season, only four teams have won the trophy, none of them ever managed by an Englishman.

Two, in fact, were Scots. Under Alex Ferguson, Manchester United won in 1993, 1994, 1996, 1997, 1999, 2000 , 2001 and 2003. Kenny Dalglish took Blackburn Rovers to their only success in 1995; Arsene Wenger's Arsenal were winners in 1998, 2002 and 2004; and Jose Mourinho's Chelsea took the honours last year.

Raith Rovers: goals, 1937–38

In season 1937–38, Raith Rovers scored 142 in 34 matches as they won the Scottish Second Division title. This is an average of over four per game. Three other teams in that division, Airdrie, Cowdenbeath and East Fife, also scored more than 100 goals; while Brechin City were beaten 10–0 on three separate occasions, by Airdrie, Albion Rovers and Cowdenbeath.

Ranger's miserable Scottish Cup run, 1903–28

After a replay, Rangers won the Scottish Cup in 1903, beating Hearts 2–0. It was the Ibrox club's fourth victory in this competition and their fans hoped for further success in years to come. Unfortunately, they would have a long wait for another final victory.

During the following 25 years the club had several near misses. They were beaten in the 1904 final by Celtic and a year later by Third Lanark. At the turn of the 1920s, they lost out to Albion Rovers in the semi-finals. In 1921, as low-price certainties, only 28,300 turned up at Celtic Park to see Rangers take on Partick Thistle. They lost 1–0!

A year later, at Hampden, they were again strong favourites, this time against Morton. There were 75,000 present; the Greenock club scored the only goal of the game and then had the audacity to ask the defeated opponents if they had any champagne with which they could celebrate. Fortune favours the brave!

Rangers' luck turned for the better in 1928. In the first Old Firm final of the decade, before the first-ever six-figure crowd in Scottish football, namely 118,115, they beat Celtic 4–0 to take the trophy home for the first time in 25 years.

Relationships

Brothers

The most remarkable set of brothers was the Hamiltons, Alexander, Gladstone and James, from the 1880s, all of whom were associated with Queen's Park, all of them capped for Scotland. Other pairs of brothers capped were:

D. Berry 1894 Queen's Park, and W.H. Berry 1888 Queen's Park

A.J. Christie 1898 Queen's Park, and R.M. Christie 1884 Queen's Park

G.R. Gow 1888 Rangers ,and J.R. Gow 1888 Rangers

E. Gray 1969 Leeds, and F.T. Gray 1976 Leeds

A.E. Hanson 1979 Liverpool, and J.A.M. Hanson 1972 Partick Thistle

J. Hughes 1965 Celtic, and W. Hughes 1975 Sunderland

J.B. Key 1900 Hearts, and W. Key 1907 Queen's Park

J.A. Lambie 1886 Queen's Park, and W.A. Lambie 1892 Queen's Park

H. Macintyre 1880 Rangers, and J. Macintyre 1884 Rangers

H. MacNeill 1874 Queen's Park, and M.M. MacNeill 1876 Rangers

D.J.F. Paton 1896 St Bernard's, and R. Paton 1879 Vale of Leven

A.S. Scott 1952 Rangers, and James Scott 1966 Hibs

M.M. Scott 1898 Airdrie, and R. Scott 1894 Airdrie

J. Shaw 1947 Rangers, and D. Shaw 1947 Hibs

A. Wilson 1909 Sheffield Wednesday, and D. Wilson Oldham Athletic.

Fathers and sons

Family Name	Father	Club	Son	Club
Battles	B.	Celtic	B.J.	Hearts
Blair	Jas.	Sheffield Wednesday	J.A.	Blackpool
Conn	A.	Hearts	A.J.	Spurs
Gibson	N.	Rangers	J.D.	Partick
Higgins	A.F.	Kilmarnock	A.	Newcastle
Simpson	J.M.	Rangers	R.C.	Celtic

Grandfather and son

W. McColl 1895 Renton, and I.M. McColl 1940 Rangers

Scotland v England: football statistics, 1872–1999

Since the first match was played in 1872, this encounter has always attracted the interest of the sporting public. The statistics of the series are as follows:

Overall record in full internationals 1872–1999

	Played 110	Scotland won 41	England won 45	Drawn 24
In Scotland:	Played 55	Scotland won 23	England won 19	Drawn 13
In England:	Played 55	Scotland won 18	England won 26	Drawn 11

Largest Scottish victory
7–2 in 1878   First Hampden Park
6–1 in 1881   Kennington Oval

Largest English victory
9–3 in 1961   Hampden Park

Scotland v England venues
Hamilton Crescent, First Hampden, Cathkin Park, Second Hampden, Ibrox Park, Celtic Park, Hampden Park

England v Scotland venues
Kennington Oval, Bramall Lane, Ewood Park, Richmond, Goodison Park, Crystal Palace, Villa Park, St James Park, Stamford Bridge, Old Trafford, Wembley Stadium

Hat-trick by a Scotland player in any full England international
On six occasions; J McDougall (1878), G Ker (1880), J Smith (1881 & 1883), RS McColl (1900) and Alec Jackson (1928)

Highest attendance in Scotland
149,547 at Hampden Park in 1937

Highest attendance in England
100,000 at Wembley in 1979

Scotland v England: the record

After the first meeting in 1872, which ended in a 0–0 draw, Scotland lost to England the following year at Oval. However, in the following 10 years, Scotland won 8, drew 1 and lost 1.

All in, there have been 110 meetings between the two rivals, of which England have won 45, Scotland 41, with 2 draws.

Scotland v Ireland for the first time

Scotland were playing their twentieth international match when they first met Ireland, in Ballynafeigh Park, Belfast on 26 January 1884. That turned out to be a good year for the Scots, as once they had beaten Ireland 5–0, they went on to beat England 1–0 and Wales 4–1.

Team: Inglish (Kilmarnock), Forbes (Vale of Leven), Arnott (Queen's Park), Graham (Annbank), Fulton (Abercorn), Brown (Dumbarton),

Thomson (Rangers), Gossland (Rangers), Goudie (Abercorn), Harrower (Queen's Park), McAuley (Arthurlie).

Scorers: Goudie (60), Harrower (12,86), Gossland (30,70).

Scotland v Ireland 11–0: biggest win, 1901

A crowd of 15,000 were present at Celtic Park on 23 February 1901, to see Scotland run up their biggest ever score against Ireland. Five up at half-time, the Scots went on to record an 11–0 win. This was also Scotland's biggest ever victory in an international.

Team: McWattie (Queen's Park), Smith (Rangers), Battles (Celtic), Russell (Celtic), Anderson (Kilmarnock), Robertson (Everton), Campbell (Rangers), Campbell (Celtic), Hamilton (Rangers), MacMahon (Celtic), Smith (Rangers). *Scorers:* MacMahon (6, 15, 40, 50), Russell (25), Campbell (Celtic; 30, 65), Hamilton (55, 60, 70, 80).

Scotland v Ireland (Northern Ireland from the early 1920s)

The first of these was played in 1884, the last in 1992. The overall record is as follows:

Matches played: Scotland won 61; Ireland won 15; Drawn 16

Biggest Scotland victory: 11–0 1901 Hampden; 10–2 1888 Belfast

Biggest Ireland victory: 2–0 1903 Hampden; 2–0 1947 Belfast; 2–0 1983 Belfast

Most unusual venue: Dublin: in 1904, 1906, 1908 & 1913; Tynecastle Park, Edinburgh 1935; Pittodrie Park, Aberdeen 1937

Scotland v Wales: first time

After a yearly match against England since the encounter in 1872, the Scottish authorities added Wales to their list of opponents for the first time in 1876.

The match was held at Hamilton Crescent in Glasgow on 25 March and resulted in a 4–0 win to Scotland.

Team: McGeoch (Dumbreck), Taylor (Queen's Park), Neill (Queen's Park), Kennedy (Eastern), Campbell (Queen's Park), Highet (Queen's Park), Ferguson (Vale of leven), Lang (Clydesdale), McKinnon (Queen's Park), M. McNeil (Rangers), H. McNeil (Queen's Park).

Scorers: Ferguson (40), Lang (48), McKinnon (53), H. McNeill (70).

Scotland v Wales 9–0

In the long series of matches between Scotland and Wales, which first started in 1876, the highest score in Scotland's favour came in 1878, when they won 9–0. The match was played at First Hampden Park in Glasgow on 23 March 1878. Six thousand were present to enjoy the goal feast. Scotland were six up at half-time.

Team: Parlane (Vale of Leven), Neill (Queen's Park), Duncan (Alexandra Athletic), Phillips (Queen's Park), Davidson (Queen's Park), Lang (Clydesdale), Weir (Queen's Park), Watson (Rangers), Campbell (Queen's Park), Ferguson (Vale of Leven), Baird (Vale of Leven).

Scorers: Campbell (4, 18), Weir (15, 42), Baird (37), Ferguson (38, 50), Watson (60), Lang (70).

Scotland v Wales: football statistics, 1876–2004

The first match in this series took place in 1876; the most recent in the spring of 2004. The overall record reads:

Matches played
103: Scotland won 60, Wales 20, Drawn 23

Biggest victory for Scotland
9–0 1878 First Hampden Park
8–1 1885 Wrexham

Biggest victory for Wales
4–0 2004 Cardiff

Most unusual venue

St Mirren Park, Paisley 1923

Scotland's first goal in World Cup Finals

Scotland first reached a World Cup Finals in 1954, but it proved an unhappy episode in Switzerland as the team lost its two matches, 0–1 to Austria and 0–7 to Uruguay.

Reaching the Finals of the 6th World Cup in Sweden in 1958, Scotland played three first-round matches against Yugoslavia, Paraguay and France. In Vasteras, on 8 June, the national side drew 1–1 against the Slavs, with Jimmy Murray of Hearts scoring Scotland's goal, thus becoming the first to score for the country in a World Cup Finals.

N.B. However, the first Scots-born player to score in the World Cup was Jimmy Brown, born at Kilmarnock in 1908, who scored for the USA against Argentina in a semi-final of the 1930 World Cup.

Scotland's international football team: foreign tour, 1928

Until 1929, Scotland's international football team had only ever played England, Ireland or Wales. Then, at the end of season 1928–29, Scotland went on tour for the first time, playing Holland, Germany and, first of all, Norway:

26 May 1929: Bergen – Norway 3, Scotland 7

Team: McLaren (St Johnstone), Crapnell (Airdrie), Nibloe (Kilmarnock), Imrie (St Johnstone), A. Craig (Motherwell), T. Craig (Rangers), Nisbet (Ayr), Cheyne (Aberdeen), McCrae (St Mirren), Rankin (St Mirren), Howe (Hamilton). *Scorers*: Cheyne 3, Nisbet 2, T. Craig, Rankin.

A promising start. The travelling party then left for Berlin by train for their next challenge. The Germans had a good side and would only decide to miss out on the first World Cup a year later in Uruguay, on account of the travelling involved. Five years later, in the Second World Cup, held in Italy, they finished third.

1 June 1929: Berlin – Germany 1, Scotland 1

For this match, the Scottish selectors made three changes. Nibloe, A. Craig and Howe dropped out and were replaced by Gray (Rangers), Morton (Kilmarnock) and Fleming (Rangers). Imrie scored Scotland's only goal.

4 June 1929: Rotterdam – Holland 0, Scotland 2

The next destination was Holland, a country at that time desperate to host the first World Cup. When all the European countries were passed over in favour of Uruguay, perhaps pique was their reason for refusing to travel. Still, the country had a good team at the time, so this was an excellent win for Scotland, with a slightly re-arranged side. Nibloe came in for Crapnell, A. Craig for Imrie and Howe for McCrae. The goals came from Fleming and Rankin.

Scotland then went on to play, away from home, France in 1930, Austria, Italy and Switzerland in 1931, and France again in 1933. Also, in 1933, there arrived the first foreign side to play in Scotland. A strong Austrian team touched down in Glasgow for a match at Hampden Park.

Although only four years had passed since that successful first tour in the summer of 1929, not a single player from those three matches made the side for the Austrian game. *Team:* Kennaway (Celtic), Anderson (Hearts), McGonagle (Celtic), Meiklejohn (Rangers), Watson (Blackpool), Brown (Rangers), Ogilvie (Motherwell), Bruce (Middlesborough), McFadyen (Motherwell), McPhail (Rangers), Duncan (Aberdeen).

At Hampden 62,000 turned up to see the visitors with the good reputation. They were not disappointed. Scotland got off to a great start through Davie Meiklejohn in only five minutes, but the Austrians showed their class to pull level by the interval.

After only four minutes of the second period, Willie McFadyen put Scotland ahead again, rather against the run of play thus far. The visitors were not to be denied a draw, however, and duly scored the necessary goal. Still, a 2–2 result against one of the finest teams in Europe was a good achievement by the Scots.

29 November: Scotland 2, Austria 2

Scotland's World Cup record, 1957–2002

Scotland's first attempt to qualify for the finals stage of a World Cup came in 1950, when Brazil was the host nation. The Home International Championship was chosen as a qualifying group, with both the winners and the runners-up being entitled to travel to South America.

The first two matches went well, Scotland beating Northern Ireland 8–2 in Belfast, and Wales 2–0 at Hampden, both in late 1949. Unfortunately, at that same latter venue, on 15 April 1950, Scotland went down 0–1 to England. That left them in second place in the table but the SFA had decided they would only go as winners and declined the invitation. In the event, only thirteen countries made the trip to Brazil: six from Europe, five from South America, Mexico and the USA.

1954, Switzerland
    Scotland qualified but were eliminated in the first round
    Austria 1 Scotland 0
    Uruguay 7 Scotland 0

1958, Sweden
    Scotland qualified but were eliminated in the first round
    Scotland 1 Yugoslavia 0
    Scotland 2 Paraguay 3
    Scotland 1 France 2

1962, Chile
    Scotland did not qualify

1966, England
    Scotland did not qualify

1970, Mexico
    Scotland did not qualify

1974, West Germany
    Scotland qualified but were eliminated in the first round
    Scotland 2 Zaire 0
    Scotland 0 Brazil 0
    Scotland 1 Yugoslavia 1

	P	W	D	L	F	A	Pts
Yugoslavia	3	1	2	0	10	1	4
Brazil	3	1	2	0	3	0	4
Scotland	3	1	2	0	3	1	4
Zaire	3	0	0	3	0	14	0

1978, Argentina

Scotland qualified but were eliminated in the first round
Scotland 1 Peru 3
Scotland 1 Iran 1
Scotland 3 Holland 2

	P	W	D	L	F	A	Pts
Peru	3	2	1	0	7	2	5
Holland	3	1	1	1	5	3	3
Scotland	3	1	1	1	5	6	3
Iran	3	0	1	2	2	8	1

1982, Spain

Scotland qualified but were eliminated in the first round
Scotland 5 New Zealand 2
Scotland 1 Brazil 4
Scotland 2 Soviet Union 2.

	P	W	D	L	F	A	Pts
Brazil	3	3	0	0	10	2	6
Soviet Union	3	1	1	1	6	4	3
Scotland	3	1	1	1	8	8	3
New Zealand	3	0	0	3	2	12	0

1986, Mexico

Scotland qualified but were eliminated in the first round
Scotland 0 Denmark 1
Scotland 1 West Germany 2
Scotland 0 Uruguay 0

	P	W	D	L	F	A	Pts
Denmark	3	3	0	0	9	1	6
West Germany	3	1	1	1	3	4	3
Uruguay	3	0	2	1	2	7	2
Scotland	3	0	1	2	1	3	1

1990, Italy

Scotland qualified but were eliminated in the first round
Scotland 0 Costa Rica 1
Scotland 2 Sweden 1
Scotland 0 Brazil 1

	P	W	D	L	F	A	Pts
Brazil	3	3	0	0	4	1	6
Costa Rica	3	2	0	1	3	2	4
Scotland	3	1	0	0	2	3	2
Sweden	3	0	0	3	3	6	0

1994, USA

Scotland failed to qualify

1998, France

Scotland qualified but were eliminated in the first round
Scotland 1 Brazil 2
Scotland 1 Norway 1
Scotland 0 Morocco 3

	P	W	D	L	F	A	Pts
Brazil	3	2	0	1	6	3	6
Norway	3	1	2	0	5	4	5
Morocco	3	1	1	1	5	5	4
Scotland	3	0	1	2	2	6	1

2002, Japan/South Korea

Scotland failed to qualify

Scottish fans help fill the coffers

On 21 May 1904, representatives from Belgium, France, Holland, Denmark, Spain, Sweden and Switzerland met in Paris and founded FIFA.

Scotland first became affiliated to FIFA in 1910 but it proved a rocky passage: in 1920 they withdrew; by 1924, the country was re-afffiliated, but by 1928 they had again pulled out.

The first three World Cups of 1930 (held in Uruguay), 1934 (Italy) and 1938 (France) went ahead without representation from any of the home countries. Because of the Second World War a 12-year gap occurred before the next one, again in South America, but this time in Brazil (1950).

By that date, Scotland, like the other four home nations, had returned to the FIFA fold. In fact, the governing body was delighted to have them back again, well aware that post-war crowds in Britain were immense.

FIFA decided to acknowledge the home nations' return by hosting a special match, where a Great Britain combined side would play one representing the Rest of Europe. The FIFA officials then came up with a very cute ploy. Well aware that the finances of the governing body could do with a boost, they decided that the biggest stadium in Europe, Hampden Park, should host the event, also expecting that the fervent Scots fans would support the match.

Around Britain, there was great excitement, not only about the match but also concerning the team selection, with various names being bandied about. In the end the selectors went for; Swift (England), Hardwick (England), Hughes (Wales), McAuley (Scotland), Vernon (N. Ireland), Burgess (Wales), Matthews (England), Mannion (England), Lawton (England), Steele (Scotland), Liddell (Scotland).

Critics across the Channel were not hopeful about the success of the 'Rest of Europe'. It was felt that the team was not as strong as it might have been, as certain countries declined FIFA's offer to send players to the trial match in Rotterdam or even permit their players to be considered for selection for the Hampden game.

In the event, the following team was chosen: Di Rui (Italy), Petersen (Denmark), Steffen (Switzerland), Carey (Eire, captain), Parola (Italy), Ludl (Czechoslovakia), Lembrechts (Belgium), Gren (Sweden), Nordahl (Sweden), Wilkes (Holland), Praest (Denmark).

A crowd of 135,000 packed into Hampden on 10 May 1947, ready to roar on the GB side; but, to be honest, their efforts were scarcely needed. After Nordahl had missed three 'sitters' in the first twenty minutes, the GB side took control and never let the 'Rest' back into it. Two goals by Mannion (1 penalty), plus one each for Steele and Lawton, gave Great Britain a 4–1 lead, Nordahl getting the goal for the Rest of Europe. After the interval, an o.g. by Parola and a goal for Lawton near the end gave GB a 6–1 victory.

It had been a good night for everyone. The huge crowd had enjoyed the football; they had seen the 'home' side win comfortably, the match had been played in a competitive but sporting manner, and FIFA were delighted that such a huge crowd of Scots should have paid so much money into their coffers.

Scots whistlers, 1960s–70s

Of the 51 European Cup finals or Champions League finals to date, on only 1 occasion has a Scottish referee handled the match. In 1960, when the final between Real Madrid and Eintracht Frankfurt was held at Hampden, Jack Mowat was the man-in-the-middle.

Of the 39 European Cup-Winners' Cup finals between 1961 and 1999, Scottish referees were in charge of 2. Tom Wharton handled the Athletico Madrid v Fiorentina final of 1962 (but not the replay); while Bobby Davidson controlled the 1975 final between Dynamo Kiev and Ferencvaros.

And after the UEFA Cup final became a one-off game in 1998 (after 39 years of two-legged matches, Hugh Dallas took charge of the 1999 final between Parma and Marseilles.

Scottish football begins

The 3 March 1873 was a momentous day in the history of Scottish football. On that Monday, in the advertisement columns of the *North British Daily Mail*, the following notice appeared:

It has been proposed by the committee of the Queen's Park club that Scotch [sic] clubs playing Association rules should subscribe for a cup to be played annually, and retained for a year by the winning team, the competition to begin next season. Scotch clubs who may wish to join this movement are invited to send two representatives to a meeting to be held to consider the matter in Dewar's Hotel, 11 Bridge Street, Glasgow, on the evening of Thursday the 13 inst. at eight o'clock.

The meeting was duly held that Thursday, and seven clubs were represented. They were Queen's Park, Clydesdale, Vale of Leven, Dumbreck, Third Lanark Volunteer Reserves, Eastern and Granville. Kilmarnock sent a letter indicating their willingness to join. These eight clubs that night formed the Scottish Football Association.

Scottish women to the fore

In the 17th century, both sexes seemed to have an interest in what passed for football at the time.

An entry in the minutes of the kirk session in Carstairs in 1628 reads: 'The minister has occasion to complain of the insolent behaviour of his parishioners, both men and women, in footballing instead of observing Sunday as a solemn day devoted to God.' That particular minister sounds like a bit of a spoilsport, just because the numbers of his congregation were down on that Sunday! He also reported women playing golf at that period as well.

However, it was thanks to the ministers of Scotland – who contributed to the nation's Statistical Account – that we know of the first recorded fixture involving only women. That took place in 1795, when the married and unmarried fishwives of Fisherow played each other in Inveresk, Midlothian.

Seniors and juniors do a 'double', 1903

When Scotland travelled down to Brammall Lane in Sheffield on 4 April 1903 for the clash with England, they took with them a support of some 6,000, which helped push the attendance up to 36,000.

After going into the half-time break 0–1 down, Scotland rallied in the second half, goals by Finlay Speedie of Rangers in the 57th minute and

Bobby Walker of Hearts giving them a 2–1 win. It was our first win since the turn of the new century.

Back in Glasgow, on the same afternoon, Scotland's junior team met England at Celtic Park. There were 20,000 present to see 'Wee Scotland' also win 2–1, the goals coming from Thomson (Parkhead) and Bennett (Rutherglen Glencairn). Gate receipts totalled £545, a record at the time for a junior clash.

That same Alec Bennett went on to have a most unusual career as a senior player, starring for Celtic between 1903 and 1908; and then for Rangers from 1908 to 1917.

His grandson, Sandy Carmichael, played 50 times for the Scotland national rugby team and twice toured with the British Lions.

Shipwrecked on tour: Raith Rovers, 1922

There cannot be many clubs which can claim a shipwreck in their history but Raith Rovers is certainly one.

At the end of season 1921–22, Raith had finished third in the First Division Championship, behind Celtic and Rangers, and a grateful Board of Directors rewarded the players with a tour to the Canary Islands.

The party of thirteen players and seven officials was in good humour as they boarded the steamer *Highland Loch* for the journey out into the North Atlantic. After dinner on 30 June, there would no doubt have been some high jinks among the players, card schools would have started and the singers would have gathered together. Eventually though, at some specific time, the manager and trainer, well aware that matches were to be played in the following few days, would have declared the evening at an end and sent them all to bed.

Unfortunately, in the early hours of the morning, everyone's beauty sleep was badly interrupted as the *Highland Loch* became grounded on some rocks just off the port of Currubedo. The cry went up for everyone to take to the lifeboats and the players joined the throng waiting to go down the rope ladders to the vessels, many still in their night-clothes.

In the days following, the newspapers at home tended to make light of the incident, but once the steamer had limped into the port of Vigo, divers who examined the vessel reported serious damage. The forepeak received the worst blow, with part of the bulkhead broken to the extent of 18 yards long and several feet wide, and the port bilge keels had been torn away.

Thankfully, all the passengers were saved and taken to Vigo, where accommodation was found for them all. The next day – July 2 – the Raith Rovers' party was picked-up by a P&O liner to continue the journey to the Canary islands. Showing true Scottish determination, the team won all four of their matches on the tour, beating Vigo 3–1, Victoria Las Palmas 4–0, Grand Canaria 5–1 and Marino 2–1.

Sine die: Willie Woodburn, 1930s–50s

There can be little doubt that Willie Woodburn was one of the best centre-halves ever to play in Scotland.

He joined Rangers in the late 1930s, made his debut in season 1938–39 and held the position for the following sixteen years. In that time, Willie collected five League Championship medals, four Scottish Cup medals and two in the League Cup, as well as collecting twenty-four Scottish Caps.

Noted for the authority of his play and the timing of his every move, Willie Woodburn was also bedevilled by an aggressive temper. Like any other player in that position, he tackled firmly but, unlike others, Willie could easily slip into a different mode – one of irrationality – when he became more of a fighting man than a footballer.

Curiously, his temper seemed to increase in intensity with maturity rather than decrease. His first ordering-off came in his eleventh season as a pro, in August 1948, when had a bitter exchange with Davie Mather, the Motherwell centre-forward, and was suspended for 14 days.

In March 1953, Willie was sent off for a foul on Billy McPhail of Clyde and banned for 21 days; only 6 months later, he was expelled from a Rangers–Stirling Albion match and received a 6-week ban, this time with the added warning that 'a very serious view would be taken of any subsequent offence'. Unfortunately, Willie never heeded the advice.

Strangely, Stirling Albion were again the opponents almost a year later, on 28 August 1954; the other player involved was Alec Paterson, the club's inside left. The incident that caused the problems was fairly minor, one of those flash-point clashes that occur in every game. The official report from the referees' committee described the action in fairly clinical wording: 'When the game was almost finished, Paterson, lying on the ground, caught Woodburn round the legs. As Paterson rose, Woodburn went towards him and struck him with his fist. When Woodburn was called, he explained that he felt a jab of pain on his knee and lost his temper.'

The whole of the Scottish game expected Woodburn to receive a long sentence. However, they were all stunned by the SFA's decision that he should be suspended *sine die*, an outcome only reached on the casting vote of the chairman of the referee's committee, John Robbie of Aberdeen. When the Scottish Players' Union sought the advice of John Cameron, QC – later Lord Cameron – the advocate's opinion made it clear that if Woodburn went to the law, he had a strong chance of having the verdict overturned. But the Rangers player declined to do so, erroneously believing that the SFA would relent.

In the event, the football authority did, but not until April 1957, by which time Woodburn had realised he couldn't play at the top level any more, and retired.

When we take into account the disciplinary records of more than a few players today, it does seem a bit over the top to ban a man *sine die* for only four orderings-off. Perhaps the authorities were worried about the red mist descending more and more as Woodburn's career ran to a close. In any case, he remains the highest profiled example of a player suspended *sine die*.

The amateurs keep their place: Queen's Park, 1867–1930

On 9 July 1867 a number of gentlemen met on the south side of Glasgow for the purpose of forming a football club. They called it Queen's Park, after the area in which the meeting was held, and the club became the forerunner of many others in what became the national game.

For the following five years, fixtures were few and haphazard. They were invited to take part in the inaugural FA Cup in 1872 and were also promised exemption to the semi-finals if they took part. This they did, the members clubbing together to raise the travelling money. A draw with Wanderers entitled them to a replay but they lacked the resources to stay on, so withdrew.

That game in London put the name of Queen's Park on the map and they kept up the momentum:

1874   Queen's Park win the inaugural Scottish Cup by beating Clydesdale 2–0. The club went on to repeat the feat in 1875, 1876, 1880, 1881, 1882, 1884, 1886, 1890 and 1893; a total of 10 wins, which puts Queen's Park third in the all-time list, after the Old Firm.

1884   Queen's Park lose 1–2 to Blackburn Rovers in the final of the FA Cup at the Oval, before a crowd of 4,000.

1885   At the same venue, and against the same opponents, Queen's Park again lost in the FA Cup final, this time by 0–2, with 12,000 watching.

1898   Queen's Park become the first Scottish club to travel to the European mainland, taking part in a 'Carnival of Sports and Gymnastics' in Copenhagen, Denmark.

1923   Queen's Park win the Scottish 2nd Division championship, a feat they repeated in 1956 and 1981.

1930   For a Scottish Cup 1st-round tie against Rangers on 18 January, a crowd of 95,772 turned up at Hampden Park, a record for a match involving an amateur club.

In spite of repeated suggestions that amateur clubs have no place in the Scottish game today, Queen's Park are still there.

Stastistics of the Scottish teams

See end of section (p. 116).

The Baker Boys

From the change in the offside law in 1925 until the early 1960s, the style of British football hardly changed. The team was announced as one goalkeeper, two full-backs, three half-backs and five forwards but played the system known as the W/M formation, although few players would have realised that.

Goalkeepers could be charged, centre-halves were of the 'stopper' variety, full-backs seldom crossed the halfway line and the stars of the team were the centre-forwards, or in modern parlance, 'strikers'.

At that time, two of these centre-forwards who graced the Scottish game were brothers, the Baker Boys. Unfortunately, neither was a Scot. The older, Gerry, had been born in New York in 1938, while Joe came into the world at Liverpool in 1940. A strange set-up, but then that's what happens when your dad is in the Merchant Navy.

Both boys were prolific goal-scorers during their careers and represented their respective countries. Their right to be included in any series of the unusual, though, concerns two cup ties just over a year apart.

Gerry was the first into action on 30 January 1960, when he turned out for St Mirren against Glasgow University in a Scottish Cup first-round tie. As might have been expected, the goals rained in against the unfortunate students, with Gerry the main culprit.

Fifteen minutes from the end, after he knocked in his ninth goal, a team-mate reminded him that the Scottish record was thirteen and told him to keep going. Thirty seconds later, as he raced on to a through pass the students' goalkeeper came out and hit Gerry full on the 'privates' with the ball, which ricochetted into the goal.

In spite of his team-mates urging to go for the record, Gerry had had enough and staggered off with ten goals to his name from a final score of 15–0.

A little over a year later, in a Scottish Cup second-round tie on 11 February 1961 at Easter Road against Peebles Rovers, little brother Joe stamped his class on the proceedings. With only ten minutes left Hibs were leading 15–1 and the majority of their fans in the crowd of 10,453 were baying for more. When Hibs were awarded a penalty, Joe Baker, already with 9 goals to his credit, stepped forward confidently but unfortunately missed, thus failing to match his brother's tally. Mind you, 19 goals between them in 2 games was not bad going.

For the Scottish goal-scoring record in one match, see below.

The biggest-ever crowd for a League match

Glasgow was particularly well-favoured by the weather for the Ne'erday carnival of football in the 1938–39 season.

As usual, the big game was the Old Firm derby, which this time would be held at Ibrox, on Monday 2 January 1939. The fans of Rangers were especially keen to see their team win this match. In the first meeting of the season, at Parkhead on 10 September, Celtic had won 6–2, their biggest victory over their oldest rivals at that time. The Light Blues' fans did not want a repeat of that!

The teams on the day were *Rangers*: Dawson, Gray, Shaw, McKillop, Simpson, Symon, Waddell, Harrison, Thornton, Venters, Kinnear; *Celtic*: Kennaway, Hogg, Morrison, Lynch, Lyon, Geatons, Delaney, Carruth, Watters, Murphy, Birrell.

As the *Glasgow Herald* reported:

> There were surprising team changes on both sides and probably Celtic and Rangers have never fielded such youthful sides. In a thrilling first half, the youths in attack – some of them debutants in that nerve-trying ordeal – were outstanding and their display of subtle, cultured and effective football was equal to the best of the great Celtic and Rangers teams of the past.

The game ended in a 2–1 win to Rangers, a good three points in the race for the League title, which they would eventually win. The emotion of the fans in the ground would have been mixed; relief for the Rangers supporters, despair for the Celtic faithful.

But once those emotions died down, they could look back on the day and boast they had been part of the biggest-ever crowd for a league match in Britain, a massive 118,567.

The first man off, 1929

The supporters of Rangers Football club were delighted in the spring of 1928 when their team won the Scottish Cup for the first time in 25 years. Their joy and anticipation were even further increased the following year, when the men from Ibrox reached the Scottish Cup final again.

By the date of the final, 6 April 1929, Rangers had already won the league, so a 'double' was on and 114,708 fans, most of whom were supporting the Glasgow side, crammed into Hampden to see the action. And action there certainly was, most of it in front of the Kilmarnock goal. Rangers had most of the play; Kilmarnock's goalkeeper Clemmie gave a wonderfully confident and competent display; and, most importantly, their left-wing pairing of Williamson and Aitken scored a goal apiece to give Kilmarnock a surprise win.

However, the incident that made the final a memorable one in the history of the tournament came in the closing moments, when an indiscreet remark to the referee by Rangers' right-half Jock Buchanan resulted in his being the first player to be ordered off in a Scottish Cup final.

The footballing young ones: young caps, 1877–1962

It is not always easy to be precise about dates of birth, so I may have inadvertently omitted some names. But as far as I can ascertain, the youngest players to make their footballing debuts for Scotland are:

	Born	Debut	Age
J.A. Lambie	18.12.1868	20.3.1886	17 years 92 days
R.M. Christie	15.11.1865	15.03.1884	18 years 121 days
A. Mclaren	25.10.1910	26.05.1929	18 years 152 days
W. Sellar	21.08.1866	21.03.1885	18 years 181 days
D. Law	24.02.1940	18.10.1958	18 years 236 days
W. Henderson	24.01.1944	20.10.1962	18 years 269 days
D. Berry	27.05.1875	24.03.1894	18 years 301 days
J.R. Gow	17.04.1869	24.03.1888	18 years 342 days
J.T. Richmond	22.03.1858	03.03.1877	18 years 346 days

The giantkillers, 1967 and 2000

The Scottish football world was stunned on 28 January 1967 when the result of a Scottish Cup first-round tie in Berwick came through.

In front of a crowd of 13,365 which turned up at Shielfield Park, most of whom were expecting a big defeat for the home side, the wee

Rangers from the Borders overcame the mighty Rangers from Glasgow by a single goal. It signalled the end for the Ibrox manager, Scot Symon.

The fans of Celtic were delirious with joy at the discomfiture of their oldest rivals. But the Rangers fans had their revenge when Celtic lost 1–3 to Inverness Caley Thistle at Celtic Park on 8 February 2000. The surprising result was witnessed by 34,389 spectators.

A headline in a tabloid newspaper on the following day summed up the evening: 'SuperCaleygoballisticCelticwereatrocious'. Unfortunately, it was not an original idea; some years before, the Guardian had the theme for a different team.

The Hampden riot, 1909

Celtic Football Club won the 'Double' of League and Scottish Cup in both 1906–07 and 1907–08. In the following season, they again won the league and the whole club was looking forward to completing a unique hat-trick of these relatively rare achievements.

For the first time since 1904, Celtic's opponents in the Scottish Cup final of 1909 would be Rangers, who had finished fourth in the league campaign behind Dundee and Clyde. Naturally, they were under pressure from their fans to stop Celtic entering the record books, so by the time both teams arrived at Hampden on 10 April 1909, the crowds were rolling up for the contest in a high state of excitement.

The result – a 2–2 draw – might have disappointed both supports in the 70,000 crowd, but any neutral would have been pleased by the tension and drama. One week later, at the same venue, 60,000 were present to see the replay, which again ended in a draw, this time 1–1.

After the final whistle, though, several players lingered on the pitch unsure about the possibility of extra-time. After some delay, they moved towards the pavilion, but the crowd, feeling that they were to be deprived of further action, erupted in anger. This soon turned into a rampant display of hooliganism, during which police and firemen were attacked, the stadium was badly damaged, and eventually parts of it were set alight.

The football authorities were not amused. Public opinion, not only in Glasgow but throughout Britain, was horrified – and wanted action!

As usual, though, little blame was accepted by anyone in authority. The SFA abandoned the tie and contributed £500 to Queen's Park for damage to their ground; both clubs were ordered to pay £150 to Queen's Park; and in future extra-time was advised in Old Firm finals.

That would not pose an immediate problem: 19 years would pass before the Old Firm met in another Scottish Cup final!

The highest-scoring day in Scottish (British) football, 1885

When Arbroath thrashed Bon Accord 36–0 in the first round of the Scottish Cup on 12 September 1885, it became – and has remained – the biggest winning margin not only in Scottish football but in the British game as well.

There was, in fact, a good explanation for the result. The team that took the field that afternoon under the designation of 'Bon Accord' was actually a cricket team, who had received the invitation to compete in error. The invite should have gone to Orion Football Club but it went to Orion Cricket Club.

The cricketers, despite arriving in Arbroath minus any football equipment, decided to go ahead with the match and duly received a real going-over. It could have been worse, though, as referee Mr David Stormont disallowed at least half-a-dozen other Arbroath goals.

Just to show how much of a mis-match the contest was, the loss of 36 goals in 90 minutes is one every two-and-a-half minutes. John Petrie, at centre-forward, scored 13 – a national record.

Almost unbelievably, while these records were being set in Arbroath, just further down the east coast, in Dundee, on the same afternoon, the second biggest score in British football was recorded, when Dundee Harp beat Aberdeen Rovers 35–0.

The kings of Europe

Surely this was the greatest club match ever played. On 18 May 1960 a crowd of 127,621 packed into Hampden Park to see Eintracht Frankfurt of Germany take on the undisputed Kings of Europe, Real Madrid, in the final of the European Cup.

Four times champions Real had dominated the tournament since its beginnings in 1955–56. They had been built into a formidable force by the President and former player Santiago Bernabeu. After building a magnificent new stadium he set about recruiting the best players in the world to fill it. From the Argentine came Alfredo Di Stéfano, the genius around whom the whole side revolved. Others who came in included the very quick left-winger Francisco Gento, a Spaniard from Santander, the Uruguayan, José Santamaría, who became the lynchpin of their defence, and the overweight but wonderfully powerful Hungarian exile Ferenc Puskas.

The Germans were a very good side. They had beaten Rangers 12–4 over both legs in their semi-final, so their reputation in Glasgow was very high. And they too had a redoubtable pair of veterans in the schemer Pfaff and right-winger Kress.

And it was Kress who burst through to put them ahead after 18 minutes. However, Di Stéfano soon replied lashing home a cross from Brazilian outside-right Canario 8 minutes later and then putting Real ahead after a mistake by the German defence. At this point the South American maestro showed his skill, orchestrating the whole game and running from box to box. Then Puskas took a hand, rifling the ball in from the by-line and after the interval converting a penalty. He then completed his hat-trick with a header from a Gento cross after the flying winger had sprinted some 50 yards with the ball. And he scored his fourth with a delightful pivot from just inside the box.

Frankfurt came back and emphasised their worth by scoring twice more through Stein, but in between Di Stéfano again stamped his authority on the game with an inter-passing move out of defence that he finished off beautifully for his third and Real's seventh goal.

At the end the normally partisan Scottish crowd gave the Spanish side an ovation usually reserved for the victories of their own national team. And for 90 minutes the only Scot on the field, referee Jack Mowat, had very little to do.

The last amateurs to play for the pros, 1933

Amateur players regularly represented the Scottish national team throughout the early years of the twentieth century. The last two players to do so, both from Queen's Park, played for Scotland in the match against England at Hampden on 1 April 1933.

The Scottish team was Jackson (Partick Thistle), Anderson (Hearts), McGonnagle (Celtic), Brown (Rangers), Gillespie (Queen's Park), Crawford (Queen's Park), Marshall (Rangers), McGrory (Celtic), McPhail (Rangers) and Duncan (Derby County).

There were 134,710 spectators present, and Scotland won 2–1, the goals coming from Jimmy McGrory in the fifth minute and also in the eighty-first.

The Old guys: first caps over thirty, 1911–52

Quite a number of players were past the age of 30 before making their first appearance for Scotland:

Name	Born	Debut	Age
R.C. Simpson	11.10.1930	15.04.1967	36 yrs 186 days
T.U. Pearson	16.03.1913	12.04.1947	34 yrs 27 days
J.T. Logie	23.11.1919	05.11.1952	32 yrs 348 days
W. Summers	14.07.1893	17.04.1926	32 yrs 277 days
P. Kerr	20.06.1891	01.03.1924	32 yrs 255 days
D.C. Coleman	14.08.1878	06.03.1911	32 yrs 204 days
A.C. Head	28.06.1902	20.10.1934	32 yrs 114 days

The Saint enters the record books: Ian St John, 1959

In 1959 Ian St John entered the record books. Playing centre-forward for Motherwell against Hibs at Easter Road in a League Cup sectional tie on 15 August, he found that the home side was in good form, urged on by the majority of the 25,000 crowd.

Much to their fans' delight, Hibs took the lead halfway through the second half, and with 12 minutes to go, were still holding on. Then St John stepped in.

Inside-forward Sammy Reid knocked the ball into the box and St John beat the Hibs' defence to it to score. One minute later, Hibs 17–year-old stand-in keeper Willie Wilson fumbled a low shot by Andy Weir and the Saint was on the spot to score his second.

And then, only half a minute after that, Sammy Reid drew the keeper out of his goal and squared the ball for St John to knock in his third. Those three goals in just over one and a half minutes might not be the fastest in Scottish football but they must be close to it.

The second Battle of Hampden, 1980

The Old Firm Scottish Cup final of 1980 was eagerly anticipated by the fans of both teams.

The league that season had been won by Aberdeen: Dundee United had collected the League Cup; so the Glasgow clubs were feeling out of things and needed a trophy to please their supporters.

The game lived up to the expectations of the crowd of 70,303, play swinging from end to end with both sides playing good football. However, no one could put the ball in the net during the first 90 minutes, so the teams went into extra-time. After 17 minutes of that, a rather speculative shot by Danny McGrain was deflected past Ranger's goalkeeper Peter McCloy by George McCluskey, the goal proving enough to give Celtic the win.

After the presentation, the Celtic players moved towards their support in the King's Park end to show off the cup. Unfortunately, a few of that huge number – in the absence of a notable police presence – jumped over the fence in their desire to congratulate the team.

That was the trigger for many Rangers' supporters to pour on to the pitch at the other end of the stadium and the battle was joined. Bottles, stones and cans rained on to the field; so-called fans pulled out iron stanchions and wooden supports to use as clubs and battles began all over the pitch. Mounted police with batons drawn galloped across the pitch dividing up the rival fans and sending them back to the terracing. The TV pictures carried those disgraceful scenes all over Britain, Europe and the world; the SFA was not amused.

Both teams were fined £20,000, but football in general eventually received a boost, as governmental intervention led to the Criminal Justice Bill being put into operation, which banned drink in sports grounds or in coaches and trains going to grounds.

Almost unbelievably, throughout all the disgraceful scenes, the players, by then back in their respective dressing-rooms, were completely unaware of the trouble.

The sporting baron: Lord Kinnaird

Among the 'names' who played for those rather unusual and unofficial 'Scotland' football teams against England in the early 1870s were eminent Victorians like Quintin Hogg, W.H. Gladstone, MP, and the Honourable Arthur Fitzgerald Kinnaird.

The only son of the tenth Baron Kinnaird of Rossie Priory, Inchtore, Perthshire, the Honourable Arthur Fitzgerald Kinnaird was an all-round sportsman, who represented Cambridge at fives, tennis and swimming. In 1867 he also won an international canoe race at the Paris Exhibition.

Kinnaird played in a variety of positions on the football field; with both the Old Etonians and the Wanderers, he won five FA Cup winner's medals; and was also a member of the official Scotland team which lost 2–4 to England at Kennington Oval in 1873 – the first full international match staged south of the Border. His normal playing attire was apparently a jersey, long white-flannel trousers and a quartered cap; when we take into account the fact that he also sported a red beard, the overall effect must have quite impressive.

Arthur Kinnaird succeeded to the barony in 1877 and went on to become a member of the House of Lords, a Lord High Commissioner of the Church of Scotland, President of the YMCA of England and President of the Football Association for 33 years.

The tragic Hughie: Hugh Gallagher, 1920s–50s

Hughie Gallagher was one of the most gifted players of his generation and was recruited during his career by Queen of the South,

Airdrieonians, Newcastle United, Chelsea, Derby County, Notts County, Grimsby Town and Gateshead.

He started his career in great fashion by picking up a Scottish Cup winners' medal with Airdrie when they beat Hibs in the 1924 final. Shortly after, he moved to Newcastle, became captain and led the team to victory in the League Championship of 1927. He was also at centre forward in one of the most famous Scottish sides ever, the Wembley Wizards, who beat England at Wembley in 1928.

In total he scored 387 goals in 541 league games. He was also the first Scot to score 100 goals in both Scotland and England. As an international he scored 22 goals in 19 matches for Scotland. Though noted for his criticism of weaker players and often involved in some controversy off the pitch, Gallagher has been described as the best centre forward ever seen in British football. Hughie Gallagher's life ended in the most tragic of circumstances when he committed suicide on a railway line after being accused of maltreating his son.

NB.   Gallagher's record of 100 goals in Scotland and in England was matched by Alan Gilzean, Dundee and Spurs, in the 1960s and 1970s, Kenny Dalglish, Celtic, in the 1970s and 1980s and Brian McClair in the '80s and '90s.

The Wembley Wizards, 1928

The early games in the 1927–28 Home International Championship had not been good ones for Scotland.

Against Wales at Wrexham, the Scots were two goals up in the first fifteen minutes but the Welsh fought back to equalise at 2–2. Changes were made for the match against Ireland, but at Firhill, in Glasgow, goalkeeper Elisha Scott put on a wonderful display to keep the Scots at bay and Ireland won 1–0.

With just over a month till the crucial fixture against England at Wembley, the Scots fans were pulling their hair out; the selectors were not too happy either. They had two matches to help choose a team for that occasion. The first came at Ibrox on 10 March, when the Scottish league met the English league, effectively a Home Scots v England game. 60,000 were present to see the Scots lose 3–6.

And that just left the international trial, three days later, at Firhill, on a bitterly cold evening. Home Scots were matched against Anglo-Scots, the match finished 1–1 and several Anglos showed up well.

Even so, there were gasps of surprise from the crowd gathered outside the SFA offices in Carlton Place on 21 March when the team was read out. It contained eight Anglo-Scots, two of whom were winning their first caps; for another player, it was only his second cap; the forward line was particularly small, with no chance of winning a ball in the air; and the centre-forward had not kicked a ball in earnest for two months.

The full side was Harkness (Queen's Park), Nelson (Cardiff City), Law (Chelsea), Gibson (Aston Villa), Bradshaw (Bury), McMullan (Captain, Manchester City), Jackson (Huddersfield), Dunn (Hibs), Gallagher (Newcastle), James (Preston) and Morton (Rangers).

The fans' initial reaction was not enthusiastic. Players like Cunningham, McPhail and Meiklejohn of Rangers, and McGrory and Willie McStay of Celtic had been left out. For Bradshaw and Law, it was a first cap; for Alec James, a second.

By the day before the match, the fans were re-assessing their opinion. As they forked out the 25/6d (£1.27) third-class fare to the Capital and boarded the trains from Glasgow, Edinburgh, Dundee, Aberdeen and all points from thence to the Border, they discussed and dissected the game. By the time they reached London, they were right behind the team and expecting it to give the English a hard time.

The team – or at least the very small home Scots contingent – had travelled down the day before the match on the Royal Scot and made its way to the Regent's Palace Hotel in Piccadilly Circus, where the English-based players had already gathered. It was hardly the ideal base. The Scots fans kept dropping in to see the players all Friday night and Saturday morning, making plenty of noise.

On the morning of the game, the players watched the Oxford–Cambridge Boat Race, had a light lunch and boarded a coach at 1.15 p.m. for the drive to Wembley. The Scots contingent was everywhere, the pipes could be heard all over the city and London seemed to be draped in tartan. So far, they had had a great trip; but would it end in victory?

A most important asset had helped Scotland's chances on the morning of the game. It poured down incessantly. By the time the match started, the pitch was soaking, a good omen for the smaller side. After the Duke of York and his guest, King Amanullah of Afghanistan, had been presented to the players, the National Anthem was played, referee Willie Bell from Hamilton blew the whistle and the game got under way.

The playing details of this match are so well known, they need no more than the bare facts here. England's Billy Smith hit the post in the first minute with Jack Harkness beaten; Alec Jackson opened the scoring with a header in the second minute; Alec James got the second just before half-time; in minute 65, Jackson headed home the third; James lashed home the fourth 2 minutes later; and 5 minutes from the end, Alec Jackson volleyed home Scotland's fifth and his own third, becoming the first Scot to achieve a hat-trick at Wembley. England's solitary contribution to the score came near the finish, a free-kick from inside-forward Kelly.

It had been a rout for the visitors and the 5–1 victory is still in the record books as the biggest victory by Scotland over England at Wembley. It was also the first time Scotland had won at the stadium and also the only time a Scot has scored a hat-trick there. And, in terms of the Home International Championship, it left Scotland in third place, with England at the bottom and Wales taking the title.

They founded the Scottish League, 1890

The Scottish League was founded by 10 teams in 1890:

Abercorn	Voted out in 1915
Cambuslang	Voted out in 1892
Celtic	
Cowlairs	Voted out in 1895
Dumbarton	
Heart of Midlothian	

Rangers
St Mirren
Third Lanark   Voted out in 1967
Vale of Leven   Voted out in 1924

Wembley 1967

It is not often that Scotland has had the chance to beat a reigning World Champion but this happened to our national football team in 1967.

After England's World Cup win in July 1966, they played three further matches that year. In the opening match of the British International Championship, against Northern Ireland in Belfast on 22 October, England won 2–0. A friendly with Czechoslovakia at Wembley in early November – and a 0–0 result – was followed by the second match in the Home International series, when Wales went down 1–5 at Wembley.

England's next international came at the same venue on 15 April 1967, when almost the full World Cup-winning team (the only change Greaves in for Hunt) took on a Scotland eleven, desperate to knock the champions off their perch. Not only pride was at stake. The British International Championship doubled up as Group 8 of the qualifying tournament for the 1968 European Nations' Championship, and this was the first clash between the favourites for the only place.

An official crowd of 99,063 poured into Wembley for the clash and they saw Denis Law put Scotland into a twenty-seventh minute lead, which they took into the interval. England fought their way back into the game, but further goals by Bobby Lennox in 78 minutes and Jim McCalliog in 87 gave Scotland a deserved 3–2 victory.

For many fans, however, the chief memory of the match is recalling Jim Baxter playing the old game of 'keepy-uppy' with the ball as a bemused England team watched.

Scotland's team: Simpson (Celtic), Gemmell (Celtic), McCreadie (Chelsea), Greig (Rangers), McKinnon (Rangers), Bremner (Leeds), McCalliog (Sheffield Wednesday), Law (Manchester United), Wallace (Celtic), Baxter (Rangers), Lennox (Celtic).

When a hat-trick wasn't enough, 1949

As he looked around at the faces of his travelling companions Henry Morris couldn't believe his luck. It surely must be a dream! Then, as he checked more closely, he realised that this was no illusion. These were Scotland's international football stars; and in a couple of days, he would be one of them.

During the Second World War, Morris had been called up to the Royal Air Force, serving initially in England, but later in France and Italy, so he made a rather late entry into professional football, signing senior forms with East Fife in 1947, at the age of 28. The Fifers were a very strong outfit at that time and Morris was to have some good seasons with them, scoring an amazing 62 goals in season 1948–49 and winning a League Cup winners' medal in 1949–50.

Early in 1949 there was great excitement among the football fraternity when it was announced that Scotland would go to the World Cup of 1950 in Brazil *if* the national team won the British International Championship, the first game of which would be against Northern Ireland on October 1.

As the date approached, the papers all held their own selection contests. Many of the team were tried and tested, but some places were still up for grabs, particularly in the goal-scoring department. And at that time, Scotland had a plethora of good centre-forwards: Willie Bauld (Hearts), Willie Thornton (Rangers), Alec Linwood (Clyde), Lawrie Reilly (Hibs) and Billy Houliston (Queen of the South), to name but a few.

The latter, a big, bustling player, was the man in possession but when he called off injured just a fortnight before the game, the selectors chose Henry Morris to take over the role – hence his presence on the Burns and Laird steamer as it made its way over to Belfast.

The team's headquarters were in Newcastle, County Down, where the players relaxed before the match, playing golf or tennis, with a few exercises thrown in under the eagle eyes of the trainer, Alec Dowdalls, and SFA secretary, George Graham. Almost unbelievably, no ball work was done in those crucial days.

As a newcomer, Morris was also introduced to the 'Glucose Diet', brought in many years before by Dr McMillan, the Scottish medic. Many of the players, like Jimmy Mason and Billy Steel, swore that it made a considerable difference to their stamina in the last twenty minutes of a game.

About 2,500 Scots fans made the trip by boat. Others went by air, some early on Friday to witness the World Flyweight title fight between local man Rinty Monaghan and Terry Allan from London, but whenever they travelled, they were all in place to welcome this Scottish team as it ran out at Windsor Park: Jimmy Cowan (Morton), George Young, Sammy Cox (both Rangers), Bobby Evans (Celtic), Willie Woodburn (Rangers), George Aitken (East Fife), Willie Waddell (Rangers), Jimmy Mason (Third Lanark), Henry Morris (East Fife), Billy Steel (Derby County) and Lawrie Reilly (Hibs).

Scotland, and Henry Morris, could not have had a better start. In the second minute, Willie Waddell made a strong run down the right wing and his cross was met perfectly by the East Fife centre-forward to put Scotland one-up.

Before half-time, further goals arrived from Waddell (2), Billy Steel and Lawrie Reilly. The Irish pulled two goals back within the first fifteen minutes of the second half, but there was no stopping the Scots, who got a sixth goal from Jimmy Mason before Henry Morris helped himself to another couple, giving him a hat-trick and making the final score 8–2.

Yet when the team for the next game was announced, against Wales only 39 days later, Henry Morris had been dropped. And, in spite of several more good seasons, he never played for Scotland again.

But what an unusual international career to look back on; one cap, a hat-trick in that particular match, when Henry Morris also scored Scotland's first goal in the World Cup.

World Champions: Renton, 1888, 1972

Renton won the Scottish Cup in 1888 by beating Cambuslang 6–1 at Second Hampden in front of a crowd of 11,000, the biggest score ever in a Scottish Cup final, one only equalled by Celtic in the 1972 final against Hibs.

Buoyed by their success, Renton quickly arranged games against Preston North End, who were runners-up in the FA Cup final, and also West Bromwich Albion, 2–1 winners Renton in that final at the Oval in front of 19,000 people. Renton beat both English teams and went on to declare themselves World Champions.

Statistics of Scottish teams

Team	Founded	Pitch Size	League Wins	Scottish Cup Wins	League Cup Wins	Seasons In Europe	Nicknames
Aberdeen Pittodrie Stadium	1903	110 × 72yds	4 Premier	7	5	26	Dons
Airdrie United Shyberry Excelsior Stadium	2002	112 × 76	——	–	–	–	Diamonds
Albion Rovers Cliftonhill Stadium	1882	110 × 72	1 2nd Division 1 Division 11	–	–	–	Wee Rovers
Alloa Athletic Recreation Park	1878	110 × 75	1 Division 11 1 3rd Division	–	–	–	Wasps
Arbroath Gayfield Park	1878	115 × 71	——	–	–	–	Red Lichties
Ayr United Somerset Park	1910	110 × 72	6 Division 11 2 2nd Division	–	–	–	Honest Men
Berwick Rangers Shielfield Park	1881	110 × 70	1 2nd Division	–	–	–	Borderers
Brechin City Glebe Park	1906	110 × 67	1 C Division 2 2nd Division 1 3rd Division	–	–	–	The City

Team	Founded	Pitch Size	League Wins	Scottish Cup Wins	League Cup Wins	Seasons In Europe	Nicknames
Celtic Celtic Park	1887	105 × 68m	39 Division 1 and Premier	31	12	42	Bhoys
Clyde Broadwood Stadium	1877	112 × 76	5 Division 11 4 2nd Division	3	–	–	Bully Wee
Cowdenbeath Central Park	1881	107 × 66	3 Division 11	–	–	–	Blue Brazil
Dumbarton Strathclyde Homes Stadium	1872	110 × 75	1 Division 1 2 Division 11 1 2nd Division	–	–	–	Sons
Dundee Dens Park	1893	101 × 66m	1 Division 1 2 Division 11 3 1st Division	1	3	6	Dark Blues
Dundee United Tannadice Park	1909	110 × 72	1 Premier 2 Division 11	1	2	22	Terrors
Dunfermline Athletic East End Park	1885	115 × 71	2 1st Division 1 2nd Division	2	–	7	Pars
East Fife Bayview Stadium	1903	115 × 75	1 Division 11	1	3	–	Fifers
East Stirling	1880	112 × 72	1 Division 11	–	–	–	The Shire

Team	Founded	Pitch Size	League Wins	Scottish Cup Wins	League Cup Wins	Seasons In Europe	Nicknames
Firs Park			1 C Division				
Elgin City Borough Briggs	1893	111 × 72	–	–	–	–	City or Black and Whites
Falkirk The Falkirk Stadium	1876	110 × 72	3 Division 11 1 2nd Division	2	–	–	Bairns
Forfar Athletic Station Park	1885	115 × 69	1 2nd Division 1 3rd Division	–	–	–	Loons
Gretna Raydale Park	1946	–	–	–	–	–	Black and Whites
Hamilton Academicals New Douglas Park	1874	115 × 75	2 1st Division 1 3rd Division	–	–	–	Accies
Heart of Midlothian Tynecastle Stadium	1874	115 × 73	4 Division 1 1 1st Division	6	4	15	Jambos
Hibernian Easter Road Stadium	1875	112 × 74	2 1st Division 4 Division 1 3 Division 11	2	2	16	Hibees
Inverness Caley Thistle Caledonian Stadium	1994	115 × 75	1 3rd Division	–	–	–	Caley
Kilmarnock Rugby Park	1869	114 × 72	1 Division 1 2 Division 11	3	–	9	Killie
Livingston West Lothian	1974	105 × 72	1 1st Division 1 2nd Division	–	–	–	Livi Lions

Team	Founded	Pitch Size	League Wins	Scottish Cup Wins	League Cup Wins	Seasons In Europe	Nicknames
Montrose Links Park	1879	113 × 70	1 2nd Division	–	–	–	Gable Endies
Morton Cappielow Park	1874	110 × 71	3 1st Division 3 Division 11 1 2nd Division 1 3rd Division	1	–	1	The Ton
Motherwell Fir Park Stadium	1886	110 × 75	1 Division 1 2 1st Division 2 Division 11	2	1	3	The Well Steelmen
Partick Thistle Firhill Stadium	1876	110 × 75	2 1st Division 3 Division 11 1 2nd Division	1	1	3*	Jags
Peterhead Balmoor Stadium	1891	105 × 70	———	–	–	–	Blue Toon
Queen of the South Palmerston Park	1919	112 × 73	1 Division 11 1 2nd Division	–	–	–	Doonhammers
Queen's Park Rangers Hampden Park	1867	115 × 75	2 Division 11 1 2nd Division 1 B Division 1 C Division	10	–	–	Amateurs Spiders

* Includes Inter-Toto

Team	Founded	Pitch Size	League Wins	Scottish Cup Wins	League Cup Wins	Seasons In Europe	Nicknames
Raith Rovers Starks Park	1883	113 × 70	2 1st Division 4 Division 11	–	1	1	Rovers
Rangers Ibrox Park	1973	105 × 68m	50 Division 1 and Premier	31	23	45	Gers Light Blues
Ross County Victoria Park	1929	110 × 75	1 3rd Division	–	–	–	Staggies
St Johnstone McDiarmid Park	1884	115 × 75	3 1st Division 3 Division 11	–	–	2	Saints
St Mirren St Mirren Park	1877	112 × 73	2 1st Division 1 Division 11	3	–	4	Buddies
Stenhousemuir Ochilview Park	1884	110 × 72	–	–	–	–	Warriors
Stirling Albion Forthbank Stadium	1945	110 × 75	4 Division 11 3 2nd Division	–	–	–	Binos
Stranraer Stair Park	1870	110 × 70	2 2nd Division	–	–	–	Blues

Left. Kenny Dalglish gives his characteristic smile as he turns away after scoring one of his 30 goals for Scotland, this time against Belgium (see p.82). *The Herald & Evening Times Picture Archive*

Below. Dick McTaggart shows the classic right lead of the southpaw. He won 610 of his 634 fights (see p.31). *The Herald & Evening Times Picture Archive*

Opposite top. Sir Chay Blyth (on left), whose feats in the rowing and sailing fields were quite extraor-dinary, with another legend of the water, Sir Alec Rose (see p.203). *The Herald & Evening Times Picture Archive*

Opposite below. James Braid playing off a fairway lie with a wood. Note the very dressy outfits of both player and spectators (see p.139). *The Herald & Evening Times Picture Archive*

Above. Ian Black, the first Scottish winner of the BBC Sports Personality of the Year Award (see p.236). *The Herald & Evening Times Picture Archive*

Above. A contemplative Robert Millar, the first Scot to win the King of the Mountains title in the Tour de France (see p.223). *The Herald & Evening Times Picture Archive*

Opposite top. The Grand Match on the Lake of Menteith in 1979, when over 2,600 curlers took part (see p.222). *The Herald & Evening Times Picture Archive*

Opposite below. John Leslie, scorer of the quickest try in international rugby (see p.183). *The Herald & Evening Times Picture Archive*

Right. The wonderful – but eventually tragic – Hughie Gallagher (see p.108). *The Herald & Evening Times Picture Archive*

Below. Elenor Gordon, looking relaxed, comfortable . . . and quick! (see p.215). *The Herald & Evening Times Picture Archive*

Opposite top. Eric Liddell (right) winning the 120-yards sprint at the Celtic Sports in 1922 (see p.9). *The Herald & Evening Times Picture Archive*

Opposite below. Dougal Haston, the first Scot to ascend Everest, the world's highest mountain (see p.38). *The Herald & Evening Times Picture Archive*

Right. Donald Dinnie, towards the end of a remarkable sporting career (see p.6). *The Herald & Evening Times Picture Archive*

Below. Jim Aitken takes the plaudits of the crowd after he scored the only try in Scotland's Grand Slam-clinching match against France in 1984. One policeman on the left has obviously been affected by the occasion; he is supposed to be watching the crowd! *The Herald & Evening Times Picture Archive*

GOLD MEDALLISTS

Olympic Gold medallists, 1912*

Philip Fleming

Born in Newport-on-Tay, Fife, in 1889 and educated at Eton and Magdalen College, Oxford, Philip Fleming made only one appearance in the University Boat Race when he rowed at number seven in the winning Oxford boat of 1910. At Stockholm, in 1912, he stroked the *Leander* eight which beat the crew from New College, Oxford by one length in the Olympic final.

Henry Maitland Macintosh

Originally from Kelso, Henry Macintosh, who was educated at Glenalmond and Corpus Christi, Cambridge, had a poor domestic season prior to the 1912 Olympic Games. He lost to Duncan Macmillan in the 100 yards at the Cambridge University sports and in the match against Oxford, and in the AAA Championships he finished last in his 100 yards heat and did not run in the 220 yards. In Stockholm, he was eliminated in the heats of both sprints and 1912 would have been a very lean year had it not been for his Olympic gold medal in the sprint relay.

In 1913, Macintosh was elected President of the Cambridge University AC and won the 100 yards against Oxford. He won the Scottish 100 yards title before equalling the British record of 9.8 secs in Vienna. In 1914, he again won the 100 yards against Oxford before setting off for South Africa, where he took up a post of Assistant District Commissioner. After only a few months, the outbreak of war brought him home and he was commissioned into the Argyll and Sutherland Highlanders. In the summer of 1918, Captain Henry Macintosh was killed in action at the Somme.

*For 1896 and 1908, see Olympics, p. 130.

Robert Cook Murray

Robert Murray, born in Edinburgh in 1870, was the founder of the first small-bore rifle club in Britain and later served as chairman, secretary and treasurer of the Urmston Miniature Rifle Club. At the 1912 Olympics, Murray won a gold medal as part of the small-bore rifle team 50-metre event and was also placed fifth in the small-bore individual event with disappearing targets, and sixth in the small-bore individual event from any position.

William Duthie Kinnear

Please refer to the 'Various sports' section (Rowing), p. 231.

Isabella Moore

Along with Jennie Fletcher, Annie Speirs and Irene Steer, Isabella Moore won a gold medal for Great Britain in the 4 x 100 metres freestyle relay. She became the first Scottish woman to win an Olympic event.

Gold medallists, 1920

Robert Alexander Lindsay

Robert Lindsay of Blackheath Harriers was on the threshold of top-class athletics when his carrier was interrupted by the war. He had finished fourth in the 440 yards at the 1911 AAA Championships and won three Scottish 440 yards titles in the years immediately prior to the war. In 1914 he was also the Scottish Champion at 220 yards.

As a finalist in the 1920 AAA Championship 440 yards, Lindsay was selected for the relay team which won the Olympic gold medals in Antwerp. Probably his best performance, however, came the following year when he defeated the Olympic champion Bevil Rudd of South Africa to take the 1921 AAA title.

John Sewell

Born in Halfmorton in April 1882, Sewell moved to London where he joined the City of London Police tug-of-war team and eventually went to the Stockholm Olympics, where he won a gold medal.

Also an accomplished wrestler, Sewell was British Heavyweight champion in the Cumberland and Westmoreland style for four consecutive years from 1907 to 1910.

William Peacock
Peacock was a member of the 7–man water polo team which beat Belgium 6–2 in the final to take the gold medal.

Gold medallists, 1924

James McNabb
Along with team-mates Charles Elay, Robert Morrison and John Somers-Smith, James McNabb formed the Coxless Fours boat which beat Canada by one-and-a-half lengths in the final.

Eric Liddell
Please refer to 'Athletics' section, p. 9 (*From the wing to an Olympic gold:* Eric Liddell).

Gold medallists, 1936

James Foster
At Berlin, in 1936, the GB ice hockey squad won the Olympic title, with Canada in second place and the USA in third. James Foster was one of the 12-man team.

Gold medallists, 1952

Douglas Stewart
Great Britain won the Equestrian team event in the 1952 Olympics at Helsinki with a total of 40.75 pts, followed by Chile on 45.75 pts and West Germany with 52.25.

The team consisted of Harry Llewellyn, Wilfred White and Scotland's Douglas Stewart.

Gold medallists, 1956

Dick McTaggart (Please refer to the 'Boxing' section, p. 31)

Gold medallists, 1968

Rodney Pattison (Please refer to the 'Sailing' section, p. 204)

1976 Gold medallists

David Wilkie

Wilkie arrived at the Montreal Olympics with three World, two European and two Commonwealth titles already to his name.

He had started the 1976 season by becoming the first Briton ever to win an American Championship title. In fact, he won three, the 100- and 200-metres breast stroke and the 22-metres medley.

In Montreal, his first event finished in disappointment, when he finished second to arch-rival John Hencken of the USA in the 100 metres. He faced the same opponent in the final of the 200 metres, and as they turned for the last length, the pair were on level terms. Coming down the final straight, however, Wilkie's superior strength told and he pulled away to win the gold in world-record time.

Gold medallist, 1980

Alan Wells (Please refer to the 'Athletics' section, p. 3)

Gold medallists, 1984

Richard Budgett

A Glaswegian, Richard Budgett had competed in three world championships prior to the 1984 Olympics. In 1981 he won a bronze medal in the Coxed Pairs; and in the Coxed Fours he was placed fifth in 1982 and sixth in 1983.

His gold medal in Los Angeles came in the Coxed Fours.

Gold medallists, 1988

In Seoul, Scotland produced two gold-medallists.

Veryan Pappin from the RAF was the goalminder for the GB hockey squad which won the Olympic title for the first time since 1920; and Michael McIntyre won his gold in the Star class in the yachting events.

Gold medallists, 2000

Stephanie Cook

Born in Irvine, Cook read medicine at Oxford University. She won her gold in the women's modern pentathlon event, the first time this had been included in the Games. She was awarded an OBE in 2001.

Shirley Robertson

Born and brought up in Dundee, Robertson began sailing on the Tay. After a 4th place in the Atlanta Olympics (1996), she won a gold medal in Sydney (2000) for Europe-class dinghy, becoming the first Scottish woman to win an Olympic Gold since 1912 and Britain's first female Olympic sailing medallist.

Andrew Lindsay

A native of Portree, on Skye, Lindsay was a member of the Oxford University Boat Club when he was chosen for the GB eights squad for the 2000 Olympics.

Scotland's Commonwealth Games Gold Medallists

Bowls (men)

Singles: 1934 Robert Sprot; 1982 Willie Wood; 1994 Richard Corsie.

Pairs: 1974 John Christie and Alex McIntosh; 1982 David Gourlay and John Watson; 1986 George Adrain and Grant Knox; 2002 Alex Marshall & George Sneddon.

Fours: 1990 Scotland.

Triples: (Physically disabled) 1990 Scotland.

Bowls (women)

Pairs: 1994 Sarah Gourlay and Frances White; 1998 Margaret Letham and Joyce Lindores.

Cycling (men)

1,000 metres: Time Trial, 2002 Chris Hoy.

Athletics (men)

100 metres, 1982 Alan Wells; 200 metres, 1978 Alan Wells; 1982 Alan Wells (dead heat for first place); 5,000 metres, 1970 Ian Stewart; 10,000 metres, 1970 Lachie Stewart; Marathon, 1930 Dunky Wright; 1954 Joe McGhee; 1966 Jim Alder.

Athletics (men), continued

440 yards Hurdles, 1934 Alan Hunter; Hammer, 1950 Duncan Clark.
4 x 100 metres relay, 1978 Scotland.
Hammer throw: 1950 Duncan Clark

Athletics (women)
800 metres, 1970 Rosemary Stirling; 10,000 metres, 1986 Liz Lynch; 10,000 metres, 1990 Liz McColgan; 10,000 metres, 1994 Yvonne Murray; Discus, 1970 Rosemary Payne, 1982 Meg Ritchie.

Badminton
Men's doubles, 1986 Billy Gilliland and Dan Travers.

Boxing (flyweight)
1950 Hugh Riley; 1954 Dick Currie; 1958 Jackie Brown; 1962 Robert Mallon; 1994 Paul Shepherd.

Boxing (bantamweight)
1954 John Smillie.

Featherweight
1950 Henry Gilliland; 1962 John McDermott; 1998 Alex Arthur.

Lightweight
1930 James Rolland; 1958 Dick McTaggart.

Light Welterweight
1990 Charlie Kane.

Light Middleweight
1970 Tom Imrie.

Fencing (men)
Foil, 1962 Sandy Leckie.

Sabre
1970 Sandy Leckie.

Gymnastics
Rings, 2002 Steve Frew (dead heat with H Giorgallas, Cyprus).

Judo (men)
Half Middleweight, 2002 Graeme Randall.

Judo (women)
Lightweight, 1990 Loretta Cusack.

Shooting (men)
Full-bore Rifle: 1982 Arthur Clarke.
Small-bore Rifle: 1978 Alister Allan.
Small-bore Rifle, three positions: 1982 Alister Allan.
Air Rifle, Pairs: 1982 Alister Allan and Bill MacNeill.
Skeet, Pairs: 1959 Ian Marsden and James Dunlop.

Shooting (women)
Small-bore Rifle, Prone: 1994 Shirley McIntosh.

Swimming (men)
100 yards backstroke: 1934 Willie Francis.
200 yards breaststroke: 1934 Norman Hamilton.
200 metres breaststroke: 1974 David Wilkie.
220 yards butterfly: 1958 Ian Black.
200 metres individual medley: 1974 David Wilkie.
3 metres springboard diving: 1954 Peter Heatley.
10 metres highboard diving: 1954 Peter Heatley; 1958 Peter Heatley.

Swimming (women)
50 metres freestyle: 2002 Alison Sheppard.
220 yards breaststroke: 1950 Eleanor Gordon; 1954 Eleanor Gordon.
4 x 110 yards medley relay: 1954 Scotland.

Squash
Men's singles: 1998 Peter Nicol.
NB: Nicol also won the men's doubles with Lee Beachill in 2002, but by that time he had chosen to represent England.

Weightlifting
Light Heavyweight: 1958 Phil Caira; 1962 Phil Caira.

Wrestling
Bantamweight: 1934 Edward Melrose.

Scotland's first Olympic gold medallist: Launceston Elliot,1896

Launceston Elliot was born in 1874 in India, where his father served as a magistrate with the Indian Civil Service. The family was part of the earldom of Minto, with a base in the Scottish Borders.

In 1887, Elliot's father gave up his post and returned to England where Elliot junior, an exceptionally well-built youth, came under the influence of Eugen Sandow, who coached him into becoming a very talented weightlifter.

In January 1891, aged only 16, he performed well at the first British Championship at the Café Monico in Piccadilly, London. Three years later, at the Royal Aquarium, Worcester, he won the Championship.

Elliot travelled to Athens for the first modern Olympic Games in 1896. At that time there were no accepted rules or classifications and many varying events were on the weighlifting programme. The two-handed lift came first. After a long drawn-out contest, Viggo Jensen of

Denmark and Elliot had both lifted 110 kg, but Prince George of Greece awarded the Dane first place for having better style. In the one-handed event, Elliot asked that he might lift after the Dane, as he felt his opponent had been given an advantage in the two-handed competition.

This request was granted but proved unnecessary, as Elliot lifted 71 kg without difficulty, whereas Jensen, who had injured his shoulders in the two-handed, could only mange 57.2 kg. Scotland – and Britain – had its first Olympic champion.

Elliot went on to set four new records at the 1899 Amateur Championships and turned professional in 1905. Later, he turned to farming, first in England and then in Melbourne, where he settled in 1923. He died of cancer of the spine on 8 August 1930.

The Scottish Olympic Hall of Fame

The following are the Scots who have won gold medals in the Olympic Games:

1896	Launceston Elliott	Weightlifting	
1908	Arthur Robertson	Athletics	3 Mile Team
	Wyndham Halswelle	Athletics	400 m
	Angus Gillan	Rowing	Coxless Fours
	George Cornet	Water Polo	
	Royal Clyde Yacht Club	Yachting	12 Miles
1912	Henry Macintosh	Athletics	100 m Relay
	Philip Floring	Rowing	Eights
	Angus Gillan	Rowing	Eights
	William Kinnear	Rowing	Single Skulls
	Robert Murray	Shooting	Small-bore Team
	Isabella Moore	Swimming	100 m Freestyle Relay
	George Cornet	Water Polo	
1920	Robert Lindsay	Athletics	400 m Relay
	John Sewell	Tug of War	
	William Peacock	Water Polo	
1924	Scotland Team	Curling	Men
	Eric Liddle	Athletics	400 m
	James McNab	Rowing	Coxless Fours
1936	James Foster	Ice Hockey	Team

1952	Douglas Stewart	Equestrian	Show Jumping Team
1956	Dick McTaggart	Boxing	Lightweight
1968	Rodney Pattison	Yachting	Flying Dutchman
1972	Rodney Pattison	Yachting	Flying Dutchman
1976	David Wilkie	Swimming	200 m Breaststroke
1980	Alan Wells	Athletics	100 m
1984	Richard Budgett	Rowing	Coxed Fours
1988	Veryan Pappin	Hockey	Team Goalkeeper
	Michael McIntyre	Yachting	Star Class
2000	Stephanie Cook	Pentathlon	Modern
	Andrew Lindsay	Rowing	
	Shirley Robertson	Sailing	

Olympic Games, Athens 2004: gold medallists

Chris Hoy: 1 km cycling.

Shirley Robertson: Sailing – Yngling class.

Chris Hoy lived up to his biling as pre-race favourite when he edged out Frenchman Arnaud Tournant by the narrowest of margins, breaking the Olympic record in the process.

Hoy is now the Olympic, World and Commonwealth Champion.

Shirley Robertson's Yngling crew won Britain's first gold medal of the games. Along with Sarah Wells and Sarah Ayton, the Scot took gold for the second consecutive Olympiad with a race to spare.

GOLF

A Dynasty of Parks, 1860

Winner of the first Open Championship in 1860, at the age of 26, Willie Park Senior had an excellent record of consistency in the event. Between 1860 and 1868 he won three times and was second four times. His form then declined for a few years, but he came back to win again in 1875. Willie Park had the reputation of being the best putter of his day.

Willie Park Junior was born in 1864 and became renowned for his views on course design, Sunningdale being one of his best-known. However, before that, Willie had a fine playing career, winning the Open in 1887 and 1889 and regularly finishing in the top six. He became a leader in the design and making of golf clubs, selling 17,000 of his 'lofter' at 7s 6d apiece; popularising the 'bulger', a driver designed to correct hooking or slicing; and designing the 'wry-necked' putter, which proved popular for many years.

Willie's younger brother, Mungo – born in 1877 – was a good player in his own right but became a pioneer of golf in the USA, settling for a while in New York. Later, he travelled down to Argentina, where he designed the San Andres course.

A long walk: Sam Torrance, 1998

When he competed in the 1998 Trophée Lancome, one month after his forty-fifth birthday, Sam Torrance clocked up his six hundredth tournament, becoming the first golfer in European Tour history to do so.

Having been 28 years on tour by that time, it was reckoned that he had walked some 14,000 miles and played nearly 150,000 shots.

Andersons to the fore: 1880s–1900s

James Anderson, born in St Andrews in 1842, is one of only three men to have won three consecutive Open Championships (in 1877, 1878,

1879). The others were Young Tom Morris (Scotland) and Peter Thomson (Australia).

Willie Anderson, born in North Berwick in 1878, emigrated to the USA just before the turn of the 20th century and stamped his name on the golf scene.

His hat-trick of US Open Championships between 1903 and 1905 has never been equalled. Anderson won four US Opens in total, the first in 1901.

Colin Montgomerie

Although Montgomerie has been eight times the Number One Player on the European Tour he has yet to win a major championship or a US Tour Event or become the best player in the world.

There are, of course, extenuating circumstances. In the Majors he has been very careless on more than one occasion; he has only been an occasional visitor to the USA, and then only for the biggest events that have the strongest fields.

However, the Scot from Troon has displayed a remarkable consistency throughout his career. To win one Order of Merit title is excellent; to win eight is an astounding achievement, and one that may never be repeated.

Eric Brown, 1950s–60s

Born in Edinburgh in 1925, Eric Brown won the Scottish Amateur Championship in 1946 and immediately turned professional. He had a hooker's left-hand grip and played with laid-off woods to help his problems off the tee. Still, that did not stop him becoming a successful performer in the pro ranks, where his short game was recognised as among the best in golf.

With John Panton, Eric dominated Scottish golf for many years in the 1950s and '60s. He won the Northern Open five times, the Scots Professional Championship eight times and seven regional titles. Eric also picked up wins in seven GB tournaments and four in Europe; and was also a Scotland World Cup player thirteen times from 1954 to 1968.

He was unlucky in that most of his wins came well before the huge rise in prize money.

However, Eric Brown's proudest achievements are to have captained the Great Britain Ryder Cup team twice (1969, 1971; one halved, one lost); and to have one of the best records in the singles, where he won four out of four. In 1953, he defeated Lloyd Mangrum 2-up; Jerry Barber by 3 & 2 in 1955; Tommy Bolt 4 & 3 in 1957; and Cary Middlecoff 4 & 3 in 1959. Only three other Scots have captained the GB and Ireland (and later European) Ryder Cup side:

George Duncan	1929	Won
Bernard Gallagher	1991, 1993, 1995	Won 1, lost 2
Sam Torrance	2001	Won.

First to the MBE: Jessie Valentine, 1930s–50s

Winner of the British Ladies' Amateur Golf Championship in 1937, 1955 and 1958, the Scottish Ladies in 1938, 1939, 1951, 1953, 1955 and 1956, the New Zealand title in 1935 and the French in 1936, Jessie Valentine was the first woman to be awarded the MBE for services to golf. She was also awarded the Frank Moran Trophy for 'the Scot who has done the most for the game of golf'.

George Duncan, 1920s

George Duncan was the first Scottish winner of the Open Championship after the First World War and also the last until Sandy Lyle won in the mid-1980s. Jock Hutchison, born in St Andrews, did win the following year but by that time he was an American citizen.

One of a family of ten, the son of a local policeman, Duncan learned to play golf on the King's Links in Aberdeen. However, when he was sixteen years of age he was almost lost to golf, as he also loved football and was offered the chance to sign for Aberdeen Football Club. Fortunately, he declined and instead became professional at Stonehaven less than a year later.

Duncan moved on from Stonehaven to Wales where his continued interest in football – when he appeared for Conway FC – actually cost him his post at Carnaervonshire Golf Club. In 1910, aged 27, he showed his intent as a serious challenger to the great triumvirate (Vardon, Braid and Taylor) by finishing third to Braid in the Open Championship at St Andrews. He followed this up with wins in the Belgian and French Opens.

The First World War robbed him of his peak years when he served as a rigger in the Royal Flying Corps. Once the conflict ceased, however, he showed that he had lost none of his skill by tying with Abe Mitchell for the unofficial Open Championship at St Andrews in 1919. A year later he went one better by winning at Deal. Using a new driver, he made up thirteen shots over the last two rounds on the leader Mitchell to collect £100, the first three-figure prize in the history of the Championship. He also finished runner up to American Walter Hagen two years later at Sandwich.

Duncan played in the early Britain versus United States series and defeated Walter Hagen by no less than 6 and 5 at Wentworth. Hagen was so intent on gaining revenge that it is said that he managed to manipulate the draw so that the pair could meet in the singles in the Ryder Cup in 1929 at Moortown. His plan failed, for Duncan beat Hagen 10 and 9 over 36 holes.

Golfing hegemony, 1860s

If there is one sport and one era in which Scotland could lay claim to pre-eminence, it could be 19th-century golf.

First along was Allan Robertson, easily the best player of his time. It has been suggested that he was never beaten in a singles match. Certainly, he was the first to break 80 round St Andrews, even using wooden clubs and 'featheries'. His death, in 1858, left a void at the top of the sport and the Open Championship was inaugurated to find a successor, the intital event being held at Prestwick in 1860 with a field of eight.

That one was won by Willie Park; but a further year on, a new star emerged. Tom Morris Senior won the first of his four Opens, receiving nothing for his efforts in the first two, then picking up the sum of £6 for his victories in 1964 and 1867.

Along the way, Old Tom, as he was better known, picked up two records. In 1862, when the Championship was decided over 36 holes, he won by 13 strokes, still a record to this day; while in 1867, he became the oldest winner, at 46 years 99 days.

Morris continued to play in every Open until 1896, but only a year after his fourth win, in 1867, another Morris, his son Tom, continued the family tradition.

Young Tom Morris won three consecutive Opens from 1868, the first when he was only seventeen years of age. After his third win, he was presented with the Championship belt to keep. In fact, the 1871 Open was never held, as a new trophy was not in place. By 1872, however, the new trophy was ready and Young Tom became the first name on it, recording his fourth successive victory. He also recorded the Open's first hole-in-one at Prestwick's eighth hole in 1868.

Definitely a star in the golfing heavens: but tragedy was just round the corner. During a match between the two Morrises and the brothers Mungo and Willie Park at North Berwick in 1875, Young Tom received a telegram informing him that his wife was seriously ill in St Andrews after giving birth.

An Edinburgh golfer put his yacht at Young Tom's disposal for the trip across the Forth but before the party even embarked, a second missive brough the tragic news of his wife's death.

The brilliant young golfer never recovered from the shock and he died on Christmas Day of the same year at the age of 24.

James Braid, 1900s–1920s

In 1948, on his seventy-eighth birthday, James Braid recorded a 74 at Walton Heath Golf Club. That on its own is a feat worthy of some comment, but in the case of James Braid it could almost be expected.

Braid was born in 1870, at Earls-Ferry and first played in the Open in 1894 as an amateur. At that time, he was with the Army and Navy stores in London as an apprentice joiner and clubmaker. After some local successes, Braid became nationally known in 1895, when he halved a match with current Open champion, J.H. Taylor. Shortly afterwards he became professional at Romford Golf Club, where he remained until moving to Walton Heath in 1904.

Curiously enough, in his early playing days, Braid was regarded as poor both off the tee and on the green. At one point, though, he found a driver which made all the difference to his length; while, after the 1900 Open, when he had repeatedly three-putted using a cleek (the equivalent of a modern 1- or 2-iron), Braid switched to an aluminium-headed club, which seemed to make all the difference.

Braid was one of three stars of the era along with J.H. Taylor and Harry Vardon; they became collectively known as the Great Triumvirate. They dominated golf at that period, with Braid's personal records being quite exceptional. He won the PGA Matchplay Championship four times, a feat only equalled by Dai Rees and Peter Thompson. Even at the age of 57, in 1927, he had been beaten in the final.

However, it is as a performer in the British Open that Braid is best remembered. In a long career, he won it five times, was second four times, third twice and finished in the first five an astonishing fifteen times. In addition, Braid became the first man to break 70 in the Open (in 1904) and was also the first to break 300 in the Open at St Andrews (1910).

James Braid died in 1950 at the age of 80.

Origins of golf, 1475–1754

1475: 'Gowf' is banned by an Act of Parliament. The edict is repeated in 1490 and 1491.

1567: Mary, Queen of Scots, is criticised for playing golf within two days of her husband Lord Darnley's death.

1628: The accounts of the Marquis of Montrose show a payment of four shillings (20p) to the 'boy who carried my clubs'.

1862: First international match. The Duke of York and a courtier defeat two other English nobles at Leith.

1744: First meeting of the Honourable Company of Edinburgh Golfers.
1754: The Royal and Ancient Golf Club is founded at St Andrews.

Playing your best golf: Tommy Armour, 1927–30

Born in Edinburgh on 24 September 1895, Tommy Armour took up golf at an early age, but his career was interrupted by the First World War, during which he was blinded by a head wound.

After a six-month convalescence, Armour's sight returned and he decided to try for a career in his favorite sport. After winning the French Amateur in 1920, he boarded a ship for the US, and after a chance meeting with Walter Hagen, heading back from the British Open, Armour was fixed up with a job as secretary of the Westchester-Biltmore Club.

He turned pro in 1924 and quickly developed a reputation as a teacher, counting Bobby Jones among his pupils. In 1927, Armour won the US Open, beating Henry Cooper in a play-off. He also won the Canadian Open and four other tournaments that year.

In 1930, the US PGA was added to his CV, thanks to a victory over Gene Sarazen; and he completed his sweep of the three top trophies of the time by winning the British Open in 1931.

Armour retired in 1935 to become the foremost golf teacher of his day. In 1952, he and Herb Graffis wrote *How to Play Your Best Golf All the Time*, which has become the best-selling golf instruction book ever.

Sandy Lyle

Born in Shrewsbury but considered Scottish, Lyle was one of Britain and Europe's top golfers during the 1980s and is one of those credited with breaking American domination of golf on the world stage.

Lyle was introduced to golf at a young age. His father Alex was a teaching professional at Hawkstone Park Golf Club and had his son playing with small clubs from the age of three. Lyle had an outstanding amateur career culminating in victory in the English Amateur Strokeplay Championship in 1975 and 1977. He also played in the Walker Cup on two occasions.

Lyle turned professional in 1977 and was nominated Rookie of the Year in his first full season as a player. His first professional victory was the 1978 Nigerian Open.

Lyle won his first major, the Open, in 1985 but perhaps an even bigger highlight in his career was victory in the 1988 US Masters. He was the first non-American to win the event, a victory made even sweeter because of the intense competition between America and Europe in all aspects of golf. Lyle has also played in five Ryder Cup squads and represented Scotland three times in the World Cup.

Scots abroad? US Open Golf Championship, 1896–1927

Since the US Open started in 1895, 13 titles have been won by Scots-born players.

James Foulis	1896
Fred Heard	1898
Willie Smith	1899
Willie Anderson	1901
Willie Anderson	1903
Willie Anderson	1904
Willie Anderson	1905
Alex Smith	1906
Alex Ross	1907
Fred McLeod	1908
Alex Smith	1910
Willie McFarlane	1925
Tommie Armour	1927

Scots and the Open, 1860–1985

From the inaugural event in 1860, Scots players won for the following 29 years. The first non-Scots winner was an amateur, Johnnie Ball from England.

In 1920, the championship was won by Scotland's George Duncan, who was 13 shots behind the leader after 36 holes. He eventually won by 2 strokes after 2 steady rounds in dreadful conditions.

Scots golf fans would have to wait until 1985 – and Sandy Lyle – before another Scottish hero won the title.

The first Open hole-in-one, 1868

The earliest hole-in-one in an official tournament came in the 1868 Open Championship at Prestwick, when Young Tom Morris achieved the feat on the eighth hole.

The golfing belle: Belle Robertson, 1970s–80s

Belle Robertson won the British Ladies' Amateur Golf Championship in 1982, and the Scottish Ladies' Close Amateur Golf Championship seven times, as well as the British Stroke-Play Championships three times and the New Zealand Championship in 1971. With an unorthodox swing but good putting ability, she helped GB to win the Curtis Cup in 1986.

The golfing Smiths, 1890s–1900s

In the latter quarter of the 19th century, three golfing Smith brothers from Carnoustie – Alex, Willie and Macdonald – made their mark on the game of golf.

Willie had an excellent record in the US Open, finishing 5th in 1898, 1st in 1899, 5th in 1900, 3rd in 1901, 4th in 1902, 2nd in 1906 and 2nd in 1908 (lost play-off). In that 1899 competition, those at the head of the field were quite closely packed, except for Willie Smith, who was 11 strokes ahead, still the biggest winning margin in the competition. In 1906, his brother Alex won and they remain the only two brothers to have won the US Open.

Willie also won the first Western Open in 1899, a feat later replicated by his two brothers, possibly a record for any tournament. Willie then moved to Mexico City, where he became caught up in the revolution of 1914–15. The clubhouse at his country club was shelled and Willie was eventually found in the cellar, although in poor condition. He died shortly afterwards.

The Open Championship

In 1860, Prestwick Golf Club staged an event for leading professional players. Eight players turned up and completed three rounds of the twelve hole course. Willie Park of Musselburgh beat Tom Morris by two strokes with a score of 174.

The following year, the event was thrown open to both amateur and professional players, a move which increased the numbers competing. The first winning trophy was a leather belt heavily decorated with silver, but that became the property of Young Tom Morris when he won the Championship three times in a row.

No championship was held in 1871. The following year though, thanks to a joint effort by Prestwick, the Royal and Ancient and the Honourable Company of Edinburgh Golfers, a claret jug was designed as the prize, and that is still the trophy awarded to the championship winner each year.

Several Scots – and a few venues – are included in the list of records:

Oldest winner…Old Tom Morris. 1867. 46 years 99 days
Youngest winner…Young Tom Morris. 1868. 17 years 5 months 8 days
Multiple victories…James Braid. 1901, 1905, 1906, 1908, 1910
Youngest competitor…Young Tom Morris. 1865. 14 years 4 months 4 days
Successive victories…Young Tom Morris. 1868–72 (no championship in 1871)
Longest course…Carnoustie. 1999. 7361 yards
Courses most often used…St Andrews (26), Prestwick (24), Muirfield (15).

What goes up, must come down! Robert Allan Cruickshank

Many Scots have travelled abroad to seek fame and fortune but few have stamped their name on their chosen field with as much authority as Bobby Cruikshank.

Born in Grantown-on-Spey in 1894, Robert Allan Cruikshank emigrated to the USA in 1921 and immediately made his mark on the golfing scene. Only two years after his arrival, he tied for first place in the US Open with the great Bobby Jones. Their subsequent 18-hole play-off has gone down in Open history as one of the most renowned. For 17 holes, they matched each other shot for shot until on the last, Jones hit a 1-iron from a sandy lie over water to six feet from the flag. Bobby Jones had arrived; Bobby Cruikshank had missed his best chance ever of taking the major US title.

Still, during the following 14 years, 'Wee Bobby' or the 'Wee Scot' as he became known, won 16 times on the US Tour, as well as finishing in the first 4 of the US Open on 5 occasions. At the age of 55, in the 1950 US Open, Bobby finished twenty-fifth, while between 1971 and 1973, he matched or bettered his age (77 to 79) no fewer than 12 times in US Tour events.

In the course of that long career, Bobby Cruikshank was twice involved in incidents that could only be described as unusual, one of them a joyful experience, the other more painful.

The happy event occurred in a quarter-final tie at the 1932 US PGA Championship at Keller Golf Club, St Paul, Minnesota, against Al Watrous. At one point, Watrous was an impressive nine-up, so much in command that he conceded a six-foot putt to Cruikshank in what seemed like an act of kindness. That act seemed to rally the Scot and he pitched in at the next to pull another back.

The next two also went to Bobby and he maintained his form so well that by the eighteenth, the American was only one-up and Bobby was six under par for the back nine. The Scot also took the last to halve the match, which went into extra holes, the first three of which were halved. On the fourth, Watrous three-putted from two-feet to halve but when he did that again at the sixth, Cruikshank parred to win the hole and the match. It had been a remarkable and memorable fight-back.

The painful experience came two years later, in the third round of the US Open at Merion, Pennsylvania. Bobby was in the lead as he stood on the eleventh tee, in front of him a 369-yard, par-4 with a small brook in front of the green. After a fine tee-shot, he rather mistimed his approach and watched in horror as the ball headed for the water. To the astonishment of everyone watching, however, and to the delight of Cruikshank, the ball ricocheted off the water up into the air and on to the green. It was discovered later that a large rock lay just under the surface.

In his jubilation, Bobby threw his club up into the air, yelled his thanks to the Almighty and went on a little dance around the fairway. But he had forgotten the effect of gravity – 'What goes up, must come down' – and indeed the club did come down, catching him with some force directly on the head, knocking him to his knees.

The blow was hard enough to unsettle him, and Bobby suffered during the holes that followed, eventually recording a poor 77 to add to his first two rounds of 71 and 71. A 76 on the final day gave him a total of 295 for fourth place, 2 strokes behind the winner.

To finish fourth in such a prestigious tournament would be regarded as an impressive performance for most people, but for the rest of his life, until he died in 1975, Bobby Cruikshank must have regretted throwing that club in the air.

HOCKEY

Fitness advice

The following letter was sent by the Scottish Women's Hockey Association to selected internationalists in 1907:

> ...The Council has noticed in former years that some players, owing to being tired *before* a match, were not in their best form, therefore they must ask each player chosen to sign the following :
> 'I undertake for *two* nights before the team starts out to avoid all excitement and fatigue, such as Dancing and Theatre going, and to go to bed at a reasonable time.'

In 1924, one of the rules for international selection from the SWHA Council was:

> Possible players and reserves must be warned to keep dates free and must not play hockey nor dance *during the week prior* to an International.

Hockey just grew and grew, 1900–98

1900: the Scottish Women's Hockey Association is founded, the fourth in the world.

1901: The male equivalent, the Scottish Hockey Association, is founded, also the fourth in the world.

Edinburgh women beat Glasgow 5–1.

Scottish women's side play its first international, losing 0–2 to Ireland in Dublin.

1902: Scottish women win their first international, beating Wales 4–0 at Wrexham. They also play two home internationals, drawing 0–0 with Ireland and losing 0–4 to England.

Scottish men play their first international, against Ireland in Belfast, where they lose 0–3.

1903: First home victory for Scottish women, winning against Wales in Glasgow.

Not such a good year for Scottish men as they lose to Ireland (0–6), Wales (1–5) and England (0–5).

1905: First win for Scottish women over Ireland in Dublin (4–3).

Scottish men play Ireland at Hampden Park; they lose but are heartened by the good crowd.

1906: First international victory for Scottish men, 3–1 v Wales in Edinburgh.

1907: Scottish men defeat Ireland at Celtic Park (3–2). Several thousand turn up for the game.

1908: Scotlish men enter first Olympic Hockey Tournament. They play in the inaugural match against Germany, which they win 4–0; later, they lose to England, who go on to beat Ireland in the final. The first Olympic goal was scored by Ivan Laing (Hawick).

1909: Scottish women's first victory over England (4–1) in Edinburgh. Scottish men play France in Liverpool and win 5–2.

1912: Scottish men's first defeat of England by 2–1 in Edinburgh. England captain burns his hockey stick in the foyer fire of the North British Hotel.

1920: First visit to Scotland by a non-British Isles team, when a USA women's select arrives. Scotland win 7–1, in Edinburgh.

1930: Scottish women travel to Johannesburg, South Africa for the British Empire Tournament. In 6 weeks, they play 19 games.

1939: Scottish men travel abroad for the first time. They play the Netherlands in Amsterdam and lose 0–4.

1948: Scotland provides 5 players to the GB team for the London Olympics Hockey Tournament. GB win silver, losing 0–4 to India in the final.

1949: Just over 7,000 spectators watch Scottish women lose to England at Murrayfield Rugby Ground.

1951: In the second televised women's international, Scotland lose 2–9 to England at Wembley before 38,674 spectators.

1958: For the same fixture, an attendance of 49,428 turn up to see Scotland lose 1–4.

1969: Scotland men defeat England for the first time since 1929, by 1–0 at Old Trafford.

1972: Scotland women defeat England 2–1 at Wembley in front of 50,000 spectators, winning the unofficial Home Championship for the first time.

1973: a SWHA touring team play a first-ever match on an artificial surface against a Great Lakes XI, at Ohio University. Scotland win 2–1.

1976: Scotland men win the first Home Countries Indoor Championships.
   The Championship was also won in 1977, 1978, 1980, 1983, 1985 and 1986; it was discontinued after 1989.

1978: Scotland women play first international match on artificial grass at Limberg, West Germany.

1979: The inaugural Glenfiddich Invitation Indoor Hockey Tournament is held in Glasgow. It was held annually until 1994.

1980: Scotland men win bronze medals at Third European Indoor Cup finals in Zurich, Switzerland.
   Glasgow Western win silver medals in European Women's Club Championship A Division (outdoor) in Barcelona.

1981: Scotland enter the European Nations Indoor Cup for the first time and win silver medals, losing to West Germany in the final. Glasgow Western win silver medals in the European Club Championship A Division (outdoor) in Brussels.

1984: One Scottish player, Veryan Pappin (RAF) is in the GB squad which wins bronze medals at the Los Angeles Olympics.

1988: The same player wins gold as GB win the Olympic Hockey Tournament in Seoul.

Scotland provides four players to the GB women's side which finishes fourth – Moira Mcleod, Alison Ramsay, Wendy Fraser and Caroline Jordan.

Glasgow Western win bronze medals at European Club Championships (outdoor) held at Blomendahl, Netherlands.

1989: Glasgow Western win silver medals at the European Club Championships A Division (outdoor) held at Wassener, Netherlands.

1990: MIM win bronze medals in 1st European Indoor Club Championship held in Amiens, France.

Scotland women win bronze medals at sixth European Indoor Nations Cup finals held at Elmshorn, Germany.

1991: Glasgow Western win bronze medals at European Indoor club Championships at Amiens and repeat the feat in 1992 at Russelsheim, Germany.

1992: GB win bronze medals in Barcelona Olympics, with Scotland supplying three players, Susan Fraser, Alison Ramsay and Wendy Fraser.

1993: First appearance of Scotland senior men outwith Europe, playing in World Cup-qualifier play-off against Malaysia in Cairo, Egypt.

Scotland women win last Home Counties Championship.

1994: Edinburgh Ladies win bronze medal at European Indoor Club Championship, held at Russelsheim.

1996: Scotland women win bronze medals in World Cup Qualifier at Harare, Zimbabwe.

1998: Second World Invitation Indoor Inter-Cities Tournament held in Glasgow.

Hockey makes its mark, 1900–70

The first recorded hockey match in Scotland took place on 28 March 1891, when teams from Fettes College, Edinburgh, and Loretto School, Musselburgh met at the latter's ground. The contest was instigated by Fettes master K.P. Wilson, who had played the game on the sands at Rossall in England.

At Fettes, field hockey, using home-made sticks, had become popular in the 1880s after the finish of the football and rugby seasons. Loretto played a more shinty-like game, and shortly before the match they were disappointed to find out that the Fettes 'sticks' were longer and heavier. However, after a spying mission and a little bit of joinery work, they were ready on the day.

In this first clash between the schools, Loretto won the first-team match by 9 goals to 5; the second and third teams of Loretto were victorious; while the under-15 match was won by Fettes.

The women took a little longer to become organised. The Scottish Women's Hockey Association was formed in Edinburgh in February 1900. Teams representing Glasgow and Edinburgh met in September 1900, when Glasgow won 1–0; and in November 1901, at Inverleith, Edinburgh, North played South, the result a 1–1 draw, in front of 500 enthusiastic spectators. Unfortunately, men at that time were very sceptical about women's hockey. And many women were too, regarding the spectacle as undignified.

Shortest international appearance, 1960

When Scotland played West Germany in Duisberg in October 1962, centre-forward Jimmy Stark (Grove Academy FC) lasted only ten seconds on the field.

At the second tap of the opening bully, Jimmy suffered two finger fractures and had to leave the field. As no substitutes were permitted, Scotland played the remainder of the game with only ten players. Even so, after a tough contest, West Germany scored the winning goal only after a controversial penalty decision against the Scots in the closing moments.

The way to go: Clackmannan County Men's Hockey Club

Just before the turn of the 20th century, Clackmannan County, one of the first men's hockey clubs, travelled regularly by train from Alloa to matches in either Glasgow or Edinburgh.

In Glasgow, the team would change in the Central Hotel, then travel by horse-drawn tram or cab to Scotstoun to play the Band of Brothers. In the capital, the Rutland Hotel near the Caledonian Station was used as a changing site before the boys travelled by cable tram car to Murrayfield for a match with Edinburgh Hockey Club.

When the train was late, the players changed in their carriage and then raced out onto Princes Street, complete with bowler hats in place, to catch the tram!

MOTOR SPORTS

A long 24 hours: Le Mans – Flockhart and Sanderson, 1950s

The Le Mans 24 Hour Race is one of the most demanding in motor sports. The first race, held between 26 and 27 May 1923 was won by two Frenchmen in a Chenard and Walker. Sadly, it was at Le Mans in 1955 that motor racing's worst ever disaster occurred, when Pierre Levagh's Mercedes left the track on the forty-second lap and somersaulted into the crowd. A total of 83 people including Levagh were killed, with another 100 injured. It is the one black spot in the great history of Le Mans.

One year later, Scotsmen Ron Flockhart and Ninian Sanderson won Le Mans in a Jaguar. Flockhart was also successful the following year but tragically was killed in a plane crash practising for a London–Sydney record attempt in 1962.

Sir Jackie Stewart

Jackie Stewart started his working life as an apprentice in his father's garage in Dumbarton. His big breakthrough in his driving career came when he joined Tyrell in 1964, with whom he gained valuable Formula Three experience.

Stewart then joined BRM for a short time but soon moved back to Tyrell and into Formula One, where his skill and class soon showed through. He became World Formula One Champion in 1969, 1971 and 1973. After being injured in the Belgian Grand Prix, he campaigned for better safety measures in motor racing, improvements which have contributed greatly to the life expectancy of the top drivers.

In 99 starts, Jackie Stewart won 27 Grands Prix.

A Scots star in an American sport: Dario Franchitti

Dario Franchitti was only three years old when his father first sat him behind the wheel of a kart. He won his first race seven years later and went on to become the Scottish Junior Karting Champion at the age of eleven. Over the following years, he won more than a hundred kart races and twenty titles.

Eventually, Franchitti's talent was recognised by former World Formula One champion – and fellow Scot – Jackie Stewart. Under his guidance, Franchitti went on to win in every category up to Formula Three. After two years in the German Touring Car Championship with Mercedes, he headed for the USA in 1999, where his obvious talent, plus an impressive photogenic image, soon earned him the attention he did not receive in his home country. In that same year, Franchitti narrowly failed to win the CART circuit championship, the US equivalent of Formula One, although the death of his close friend, Canadian Greg Moore, was devastating.

Even today, when Dario Franchetti is recognised in the USA as a top name in his chosen field of motor sport, in Scotland he is better known for marrying the actress Ashley Judd in 2001.

A Scottish driving first: Jim Clark

Jim Clark was born in Fife in 1936, the son of a wealthy sheep farmer. He left school at 16 to work on the farm but spent a lot of time driving his father's Austin 7 round the fields. Later, he became seriously interested in motor racing, inspired by Mike Hawthorn's win in the 1951 Leinster Trophy, and eventually made his racing debut at Crimond Airfield, near Aberdeen, driving a DKW Saloon.

By the late 1950s, Clark's driving was impressing more than a few knowledgeable observers. He met Colin Chapman, boss of Lotus Cars in 1958 at Brands Hatch but did not take up the offer to join Lotus until 1960, when he made his Formula One debut in the Dutch Grand Prix, as team-mate John Surtees was contracted to a motor-cycle race.

Two years later, Clark won the first of his 25 Grand Prix wins, at Spa, and ended the season as runner-up in the World Championship to Graham Hill.

In 1962, however, Clark was champion for the first time, winning a record seven rounds, becoming not only the youngest winner up to that time but also the first Scottish driver to hold the title. Two years later, Clark picked up the title again; and he also became the first Briton to win the coveted Indianapolis 500 title.

In 1968, at the age of 32, Jim Clark lost his life at Hockenheim, after a crash which stunned the racing world. He had taken part in 72 Grands Prix, winning 25, along with those 2 World Championship titles.

Speedway comes to Scotland: 1928–1950s

The first-ever Speedway meeting in Scotland was held at the Olympic Stadium, Camlachie, in 1928.

The sport reached a peak of popularity in the 1950s when the White City Tigers (Glasgow), Ashfield Giants (Glasgow), Edinburgh Monarchs and the Lanarkshire Eagles raced against each other and visiting English teams. Crowds of up to 20,000 could pack into the White City and Ashfield.

The tragic two-wheelers

While the exploits of our motor-racing stars like Jim Clark, Jackie Stewart and David Coulthard are well publicised, our successes in the field of motorcycle racing are less well known. Tragically, three Scottish stars of this sport were all killed at the height of their powers.

Jimmie Guthrie, born in Hawick in 1897, was one of the most distinguished road-racing riders of the period between the World Wars. In those days, there were no world championships but Guthrie did win the highest distinction then attainable, the European Championships in 1936. One year earlier, he had set a new world one-hour record of 114.92 miles at the Montlhery track in France. Riding a Norton, he won the senior and junior TT races in 1934 and almost repeated the double in 1935, winning the junior and losing the senior by only four seconds. Tragically however, in the German Grand Prix of 1937, while well in the lead, Guthrie crashed at the last corner and died shortly afterwards at the age of 40.

Fergus Anderson continued the Scotttish presence at the highest level. He spent his peak years in the 1950s living in Italy and riding for Guzzi.

On this machine, he won the 350 cc world championship in 1953, retained the title in 1954 and then retired to take charge of the factory's competition department.

Anderson resigned in 1955 on a point of principle and decided to race again at the age of 47. Offered a BMW for the 1956 season, he crashed at Floreffe in Belgium and was killed.

In this same period, another Scot rose to fame on the road circuit on the Isle of Man. Riding a 500 cc Gilera in the 8-lap TT of 1957, the much-respected Glaswegian Bob McIntyre became the first rider to lap at over 100 mph. On his second circuit, his speed was recorded at 101.03 mph; on lap four, he increased this to 101.12 mph.

Like Jimmy Guthrie, McIntyre also set a world record for one hour, covering 141 miles at Monza in 1957. Unfortunately, while in contention for the 1962 World Championships, Bob McIntyre died as a result of a crash at Oulton Park. He was 33.

OLYMPICS

The youngest ever: Linsey MacDonald, 1980

In Moscow in 1980, 16-year-old Linsey MacDonald from Dunfermline took part in the 400-metres final, and although she finished last she became the youngest ever Olympic track finalist.

When Scotland had a most successful Olympics: the 1908 Olympic gold medallists

The fourth Olympics, held in London in 1908, was to prove a very successful Olympiad for Scottish competitors.

These games had been originally planned for Rome, but the Italians pulled out for financial reasons and the Olympiad was then awarded to London. Most of the events were held in the White City Stadium, which included a running track, a cycle track, a soccer field, a swimming pool and a platform for wrestling and gymnastics.

Scotland won five gold medals in these games, in four different sports. One came in rowing, more specifically in the Coxless Fours. Angus Gillan (later Sir J.A. Gillan, KBE, CMG), born in Aberdeen in 1885, was a member of the Magdalen College foursome which won two events at Henley before going on to pick up the gold in the Olympics. Four years later, he was a member of the *Leander* crew which won the eights at the Stockholm Games and so became the first oarsman from any country to win two Olympic gold medals.

––––––

Water polo provided another Scottish gold, thanks to George Thomson Cornet of Inverness. A member of the Inverness Swimming Club, George was the oldest of the winning British team at both the 1908 games (when they beat Belgium 9–2 in the final) and 1912 (when they pipped Sweden).

All in, George played 17 times as a back for Scotland between 1897 and 1912 and spent most of his working life as an employee of the Highland Railway.

––––––––––

Another success came in yachting, see 'When the Olympics came to Scotland'.

––––––––––

The final two golds came in athletics. The son of a Glasgow doctor, Arthur Robertson proved to be a brilliant all-round sportsman at school. After leaving, he concentrated on cycling, not taking up athletics seriously until he was 25 but quickly making his mark in the new sport.

In March 1908, Robertson won the English and international cross-country titles; while a disappointing second place in the AAA four-mile race in July still earned him a place in the Olympic Games squad.

Over a distance of three miles, Robertson finished second as an individual and won a gold medal as part of the winning team. Later, in the same games, he picked up a silver medal in the steeplechase and finished fifth in the five-mile race.

––––––––––

The other final in which a Scot won a gold medal, the 400 metres, turned out to be one of the most unusual and controversial in the history of the Olympic Games.

The Scottish – and British – champion of the time was Wyndham Halswelle. Born in London of Scots parents, Halswelle had an impressive athletic career at Charterhouse and the RC Sandhurst, before being commissioned into the HLI in 1901.

While fighting the Boers out in South Africa, Halswelle's talent was noted and encouraged, but it was not until his return in 1904 that he took up athletics in earnest. A year later, he captured the Scottish and AAA 440 yards titles; in 1906, at the Athens Olympics, he won a silver medal in the 400 metres and a bronze in the 800 metres; and on his return, he took four titles – the 100 yards, 200 yards, 440 yards and 880 yards – on the same afternoon in the Scottish Championships.

A leg injury hampered his career in 1907 but he came back to form in 1908 by setting a world record of 31.2 seconds for 300 yards. Now, in London for his second crack at the 400 metres title, Halswelle showed he was ready by setting an Olympic record of 48.4 seconds in his semi-final.

These particular games had been very well organized but had not been without some disputes. The Russians tried to prevent the Finns from displaying the Finnish flag; the English tried to do the same to the Irish; and British officialdom, occasionally a trifle supercilious, had led to protests from France, Canada, Italy, Sweden and, particularly, the USA.

As Halswelle would be up against three other competitors in the final – all from the USA –in a race run without lanes, the authorities tried to protect him by stationing officials every twenty yards.

A runner called Robbins raced into the lead from the start, and by halfway was about 10 yards clear. Then the others started to pull him back, with the other two Americans, Taylor and Carpenter, trying to block Halswelle. As they all came into the home straight close-packed, the Scot tried to run outside the other two, but Carpenter started to run diagonally, pushing Halswelle further and further out until he was only inches from the outside edge.

Seeing what was happening, the judges stepped forward and broke the tape. After a meeting lasting one hour, they declared a verdict of 'no race', Carpenter was disqualified and a re-run ordered, this time in lanes. However, Robbins and Taylor sided with Carpenter and refused to run, so Halswelle came out by himself to run a single lap to win the 1908 400 metres gold medal by a walk-over.

Soured by the whole incident, he only raced once more before giving up athletics for good. In 1915, at the age of 32, Captain Wyndham Halswelle was killed by a sniper's bullet at Neuve Chapelle in France.

When the Olympics came to Scotland, 1908

In the year 1908, there were several incidents which caught the attention of the headline-writers.

In Oldham, for instance, in early January, 2,000 textile workers went on strike for better conditions; in March, Florence Nightingale received the Order of Merit for her work with the sick; Herbert Asquith became the new British Liberal Prime Minister in April; while in the music world, the two top hits were 'Oh! Oh! Antonio' and 'Shine On Harvest Moon'.

In April too, the Olympic Games came to London. These were the longest ever games, running from 27 April 1908 till 31 October. A total of 1,500 competitors from 19 nations took part in 13 different sports, with a huge crowd eager to watch the action.

Most of the yachting events were held at Cowes, where competitors from Europe and North America enjoyed the good sailing conditions provided by the Solent. In the 12-metre class, however, there were no foreign boats entered, although some good rivalry was anticipated, as one of the two entrants was from Scotland and the other from England.

Charles McIver's *Mouchette* was crewed exclusively by Englishmen from Merseyside, while the crew of *Hera* were all Scotsmen from the Royal Clyde Yacht Club.

Rather than take both boats all the way to Cowes, the organizers decided to base the 12-metre class races on the Clyde, and so it became the only Olympic event ever held in Scotland.

A trip 'doon the watter' was a very popular pastime in those days, with many steamers providing this service, but sailing a 12-metre yacht was the hobby of the wealthy and *Hera's* owner was certainly in that category. Thomas Glen-Coats was the eldest of the four sons of Sir Thomas Glen-Coats, baronet.

Educated at Eton and Oxford, he enjoyed a life of leisure, playing no part in the family business, J. & P. Coats, the spinning merchants. Just turned 28 before the start of the Games, he assembled a crew from the RCYC which reflected the class of that establishment; John Aspin, varnish manufacturer; John Buchanan, farmer; John Bunten, mechanical engineer; Arthur Downes, doctor; John Downes, electrical engineer; Thomas Tait, solicitor; plus David Dunlap, John McKenzie and Albert Martin.

The best-of-three series was blessed with good sailing weather, and as *Hera* won the first two races, the third was not contested. In the only Olympic event ever held in Scotland, ten Scotsmen had gained the supreme prize of a gold medal.

RUGBY

Best team to play at Hampden

The specific section on Hampden Park shows just how many and how varied the football matches it hosted through the years. Yet there could be a case for including two international rugby sides among the best teams ever to grace the hallowed turf on Glasgow's south side.

Both of these were 'Colonial' sides, to use a term prevalent at the time. The first was New Zealand, the All-Blacks, who played a Glasgow and West of Scotland select on Wednesday, 22 November 1905. The previous Saturday, 21,000 had turned out at Inverleith to see Scotland lose to the visitors by the narrow margin of 7–12. There was one curious piece of pre-match controversy. Dr N. Fell, by then resident in New Zealand, who had played seven times for Scotland while a medical student at Edinburgh University, decided not to play against his fellow-countrymen and was replaced by Louis Greig on the morning of the game. Greig later became equerry to the Duke of York (later King George VI) and partnered him in the Wimbledon doubles in 1926.

For the midweek game 10,000 made the journey to Hampden, the attendance being boosted by children from Glasgow's fee-paying schools, who were given the afternoon off to see this famous side. As the All-Blacks had won their previous 20 matches on the tour, few in the crowd were expecting a home win, but they hoped that the biting and driving rain might upset the more fancied side.

Sadly, those hopes were soon dashed. The visitors' forwards – who towered over the local pack – controlled the game, showing a remarkable combination of strength and skill. They also scored two goals and four tries, which, in the scoring system of the time, gave them a 22–0 victory.

Just over a year later, on 17 November 1906, the Scotland rugby side was back at Hampden for another important match, this time against

South Africa, when a wonderful try by K.G. McLeod sealed a victory for Scotland in front of a 30,000 crowd.

However, some very fine football teams have also graced the Hampden turf, like Argentina, June 1977; Austria, November 1933; Brazil, June 1966 and June 1973; Holland, May 1966; West Germany, November 1973; Hungary, 1954; Poland, 1960; and Uruguay, May 1962. We must not forget, either, the wonderful display by Real Madrid in the final of the European Cup in 1960.

Cancellation, 1878–79, 1972

In 1878, the Scotland v Ireland match, scheduled for Glasgow, did not take place because the two Irish Unions (the Irish Football Union and the Northern Football Union of Ireland) were in dispute with each other. The disagreement ended with the formation of a single body, the Irish Rugby Football Union, in 1879.

In 1972, the deteriorating political situation in Ireland led to the cancellation of the Ireland v Scotland fixture due to be played in Dublin.

Dispute: Scotland–England, 1884–90

The England–Scotland international at Blackheath on 1 March 1884 ended in controversy when the Scots objected to the legality of a try scored by R.S. Kindersley of Exeter. Only after some discussion among the visitors was the ensuing kick allowed to be taken – a score which gave England a narrow win.

After the game, the incident was reported to the Rugby Football Association but it soured relations between the two countries, leading to the cancellation of similar fixtures in 1885, 1888 and 1889. Only the formation of the International Board in 1890 solved the dispute.

First Grand Slam, 1925

The International Rugby Championship began in the season of 1882–83 but the number of competing nations has been variable. Scotland,

England, Ireland and Wales made up the numbers initially; France were invited to join in 1910 but were later excluded from 1931 until 1947 due to accusations of professionalism among their clubs.

Up until the time of the First World War, Scotland had won the championship on seven occasions and shared it on another two. During those four dreadful years from 1914 to 1918, we lost more capped internationalists than any other country, yet we recovered well and our record in the 1920s of 25 wins from 41 matches makes it our best decade – a record likely to stand the test of time.

Some things, though, never change; the Scots fans wanted more. The Triple Crown, for instance, had not been won since 1907, and by the year 1925 we had lost to England on seven successive occasions. So it was an excited, if slightly apprehensive crowd of 20,000 which gathered at Inverleith for the last international ever played there, against the French on 24 January.

Initially, there was room for concern, as the pack lacked cohesion but the backs, all from Oxford University, soon came into their own, scoring seven tries, the legendary winger Ian Smith being the star with four. A good start, 25–4 to Scotland.

In Swansea, two weeks later, the whole team played brilliantly and the Welsh were seen off 24–14, Ian Smith scoring another four and right-winger Johnny Wallace getting two.

At the end of January in Dublin, though, the Irish proved to be much tougher customers. In soft conditions, and with a greasy ball, the forwards gave a very good display, a Herbert Waddell dropped goal sealing Scotland's victory by 14–8. That just left the finale against England to come and what a match was in prospect.

The setting was good too, the new venue of Murrayfield, and vast crowds rolled up to see it. The official attendance was 60,000, the estimated actual one 80,000, and thousands more failed to get in. Even better, the match lived up to its billings, never having a dull moment from start to finish, and again it was thanks to a dropped-goal by Waddell in the closing stages that Scotland finally triumphed 14–11.

That was our sixth Triple Crown but first Grand Slam. Rugby was certainly different back in those days. Of the season's tally of 17 tries, 14 of them came from wingers!

	P	W	D	L	F	A	Pts
Scotland	4	4	0	0	77	37	8
Ireland	4	2	1	1	42	26	5
England	4	2	1	1	42	37	5
Wales	4	1	0	3	34	60	2
France	4	0	0	4	23	58	0

First rugby match under the lights: 1879

The first floodlit rugby match took place at Hawick on 24 February 1879. The match between Hawick and Melrose attracted a good crowd of 5000 (£63 gate money) and finished in a win for the home side.

The power for the lights came from two dynamos driven by steam engines, and the illumination was very acceptable. Unfortunately, the Hawick officials switched the power off immediately the game ended and spectators were left to stumble out of the ground and through the local snow-covered streets in complete darkness.

First Scotland–England encounter with the Oval ball, 1871

The initial – and official – matches between Scotland and England at both football and rugby had the same origins.

Having been founded in 1863, the Football Association quickly made efforts to strengthen its remit. Initially, this consisted of a match between the London and Sheffield clubs, a contest which proved so popular that other similar district matches were organised.

In March 1870, the FA arranged a game at the Oval cricket ground and called it 'England v Scotland'. Unfortunately, the Scottish XI was made up only of players from the London area, some of whom had quite tenuous connections with Scotland.

However, the game went ahead and was a great success, with the England XI, not surprisingly, being victorious. The secretary of the FA, C.W. Alcock, then organised another match of a similar nature, also to be played in London in November 1970.

This time, Alcock wrote to several Scottish newspapers inviting clubs to nominate players for the Scottish side. Only one player put his name forward and England won again.

This obviously annoyed some of the Scots rugby boys because a month later, a letter appeared in both the *Scotsman* and *Bell's Life in London.*

It was signed by the captains of five senior Scottish clubs – West of Scotland FC, Edinburgh Academicals FC, Merchistonian FC, Glasgow Academical FC and St Salvador FC, St Andrews – and challenged 'any team selected from the whole of England to play in a match, 20-a-side, Rugby Rules, either in Edinburgh or Glasgow on any day during the current season that might be found suitable to the English players'.

The letter sparked off a sequence of events:

January 1871: Rugby clubs in London took up the challenge. Mr B.H. Burns, secretary of the oldest-established club, Blackheath, sent a letter of acceptance.

In Edinburgh, a committee of six was formed to make the necessary arrangements. The match was fixed for Monday, 27 March 1871 at Raeburn Place, on the outskirts of Edinburgh in the village of Stockbridge. Two trial matches were to be be held, one in Glasgow on 11 March and the other in Edinburgh on 20 March.

The team eventually chosen was as follows: W.D. Brown (Glas Acads), T. Chalmers (Glas Acads), A. Clunies-Ross (St Andrews Univ), T.R. Marshall (Edin Acads), J.W. Arthur (Glas Acads), W. Cross (Glas Acads), A. Buchanan (RHSFP), A.G. Colville (Merchistonians), D. Drew (Glas Acads), J.F. Finlay (Edin Acads), J. Forsyth (Edin Acads), R.W. Irvine (Edin Acads), W.J.C. Lyall (Edin Acads), J.L.H. MacFarlane (Edin Univ), J.A.W. Mein (Edin Acads), J.F. Moncrieff (Edin Acads), R. Munro (St Andrews),

G. Ritchie (Merchistonian), A.H. Robertson (West of Scotland), J.S Thomson (Glas Acads).

A.G. Colville had been playing with Blackheath since 1867 and thus became the first Anglo-Scottish cap. He had been invited to play for England but opted for Scotland.

J.H.L. MacFarlane had been born in Jamaica; while A. Clunies-Ross was part-Scots, part-Malaysian. Both of these players became Scotland's first 'Colonial' caps.

27 March 1871: There was a slight north-easterly breeze for the match, which started at 3 p.m. At the entrance to the ground, the organising committee set up a baize-covered table, on which stood an earthenware bowl. Spectators were expected to put their one shilling (10p) into it and Mr J.A. Macdonald, later Lord Kingsburgh, was alongside to keep an eye on the proceedings.

The pitch was fairly narrow, which seemed to impede the progress of the speedy English backs. Play was fairly even over the first-half but towards the latter part of the game, the better fitness of the Scots began to tell and they scored the winning try two minutes from the end, winning by one goal and one try to one try.

Both Scotland's scores were the result of some dispute on the pitch, but the decisions of the umpires were final, and at the whistle the home team celebrated a famous victory.

NB The umpire who awarded the Scots try was Dr Almond, the headmaster of Loretto School. In later years, he wrote an account of the thinking behind that – and presumably many other – decisions. 'When an umpire is in doubt, I think he is justified in deciding against the side which makes most noise. They are probably in the wrong.'

We start the Sevens, 1880

When enthusiasts in many different countries claim that their favourite sport started in their part of the world, others are equally quick to knock their theories down.

In the case of 7-a-side rugby, however, there is no doubt of the origin. This exciting game started in Scotland; in the Border town of Melrose, to be precise.

In 1883, Melrose Football Club was casting around for ideas to help the club's finances when a member called Ned Haig suggested the hosting of a football tournament, albeit one with a difference. Well aware of the problems of trying to accommodate various teams of fifteen players in the course of one afternoon, Haig suggested that the numbers be reduced to seven men on each side.

Whether Ned Haig meant the club to host athletic events with a football tournament or a football tournament with athletic events, we do not know. On the list of events for that first afternoon were foot races, drop kick competitions, dribbling races and place kicking but the football tournament proved the biggest draw, attracting interest throughout the Borders. A trophy was presented for it by the 'Ladies of Melrose'.

Special trains were run from Galashiels and Hawick; 862 came from the former, 509 by special train and 353 by ordinary train. Melrose saw 1600 tickets sold during the day, so by the time the event started, on 28 April 1883, the ground was packed.

The team from Kelso failed to turn up, but seven other sides took part: Gala, Gala Forest, Selkirk, St Cuthbert's, Earlston, St Ronan's and Melrose. Gala met the hosts in the final and perhaps there was something fitting about the instigators of the sport of Sevens, Melrose, winning that first final by a single try.

The tournament had been a great success and news of its popularity quickly spread. Other clubs were quick to start their own competitions: Galashiels in 1884, Hawick in 1885, Jedforest in 1894 and Langholm in 1908.

But the game first began at the Melrose Sports, an event held annually except when interrupted by war. Winners of the prestigious trophy have come from all corners of the world.

As for the game of Sevens itself, Ned Haig's idea has spread throughout the world, the developing rugby nations in particular showing an aptitude for its combination of speed and teamwork.

A lone Scot on tour with the Lions, 1888–91

The first touring British Isles rugby team made the long journey to Australia in the summer of 1888 and played 16 matches, of which they won 14 and drew 2. The squad then travelled on to New Zealand, where they played another 19 games, winning 13, losing 2 and drawing 4. Of the 20 players involved, the only Scot was Angus Stuart of Dewsbury. Tragically, the captain, R.L. Sneddon, was drowned in a sculling accident in the early part of the tour.

The first such trip to South Africa took place in 1891, when 21 players were in the touring party. It was a highly successful tour, with 20 wins from 20 matches; and 4 Scots, including the captain, W.E. Maclagen, were in the squad.

Scots everywhere

When the touring 1903 British/Irish side met South Africa in the first test in Johannesburg, both captains and the referee were Scots!

The tourist's captain, Mark Morrison of Royal High FPs, had first been capped in 1896, been made captain in1899, and led Scotland to the Triple Crowns of 1901 and 1903.

His opposite number was forward Alex Frew, formerly of Edinburgh University, who two years before had played under Morrison in the Triple Crown side. Originally from Kilmarnock, Frew qualified in medicine at Edinburgh University and emigrated to the Transvaal. Playing alongside him was another former Scotland forward, Saxon McEwan, who had won 16 caps between 1894 and 1900.

Referee Bill Donaldson had also been a well-known player, winning a blue at Oxford in 1892–94 and picking up six Scotland caps, the last against Ireland in 1899. In that match, thanks to his drop-kicking Scotland's sole penalty goal, Donaldson became the first Scotsman to score at the new national ground at Inverleith, Edinburgh.

The Johannesburg test was drawn 10–10; the second finished in a scoreless draw; and South Africa won the third to take a series for the first time. They would not lose at home for another 55 years.

First World War: deaths of rugby internationalists, 1914–18

During the First World War, which lasted from 1914 to 1918, a total of 111 rugby internationalists lost their lives. If we compare the figures to the relevant populations, there does seem to be a disproportionate number from Scotland: Scotland, 30; England, 26; France, 23; Wales, 10; Ireland, 9; New Zealand, 9; South Africa, 4.

Help from the Chief Constable

In Cardiff, on 3 February 1906, Scotland met Wales in the first of the season's internationals. Wales had won the Championship the previous season, so the Scots were keen to do well and went into the match with great enthusiasm.

For the occasion 25,000 were present with all classes of Welsh society represented, many of the better-off taking the chance to make their presence felt. One of these was the Chief Constable of Cardiff, arrayed in all his finery, walking up and down the in-goal area.

From the kick-off, the Scots took control, their pack good in the loose. Early in the match, as the Scots pressed, wing-forward 'Darky' Bedell-Sivright, a former Lions captain, noted for his dribbling powers, led a Scottish rush into the Welsh 25. He toed the ball over the line, it struck the Chief Constable and ricocheted off to one side but Bedell-Sivright quickly changed course and touched the ball down to score a try.

Unfortunately, the referee, Mr Allen from Ireland, ruled that by touching the Chief Constable the ball had 'gone dead', and he refused to allow the try. Scotland had lost a good chance to take the lead; later in the same half, the Welsh scored two tries and held on to win 9–3.

I should imagine the Scots players were not impressed by the Chief Constable. And they would not have been amused when the International Board decided that, in similar occurrences in the future, the decision should go against the team responsible for the ground arrangements.

In other words, the Scottish try should have been awarded. 'We Wuz robbed!'

Highest score in a drawn international match in rugby, 1983

When Scotland ran out at Murrayfield on 12 November 1983 to meet the touring All Blacks, the hopes and expectations of their fans were not high. In eleven previous meetings between the two nations, Scotland had lost ten and drawn only one, a 0–0 result in 1964.

Still, that did not prevent a capacity turn-out at the national stadium keen to see this Scots team put up a good performance: P. Dodds (Gala), J. Pollock (Gosforth), A. Kennedy (Watsonians), D. Johnston (Watsonians), R. Baird (Kelso), J. Rutherford (Selkirk), R. Laidlaw (Jedforest), J. Aitken (Gala), C. Deans (Hawick), I. Milne (Heriots), W. Cuthbertson (Harlequins), T. Smith (Gala), J. Calder (Stewart Melville), I. Paxton (Selkirk), J. Beattie (Glasgow Academicals).

Scotland opened the scoring, thanks to a drop-goal by John Rutherford: New Zealand drew back with a penalty. Rutherford put the Scots ahead again with another drop-goal: New Zealand replied with a converted try and a try to go 13–6 up. Misdeneanours on both sides gave chances to the kickers, three of which were successfully put over by Peter Dodds, making the score at half-time 16–15 in New Zealand's favour.

Just after the interval, the All Blacks extended their lead to 22–15 with a converted try. However, two more penalties by Dodds brought the Scots to within one point before another penalty by All Black's full-back Deans moved the score to 25–21. The Scots looked out, but in the very last minute Jim Pollock went over in the corner to level the scores. The crowd went wild with excitement, then went quiet as Peter Dodds stepped up to take the penalty which would give Scotland victory. For a second, the crowd roared its approval of his fine strike; but quickly the roars turned to groans as the ball slid past the upright by a whisker.

Even then the drama was not over. Just on the final whistle referee R. Hourquet of France awarded a very kickable penalty to the All Blacks. However, touch judge Brian Anderson drew the referee's attention to another infringement which resulted in the penalty being reversed, and the Scots could clear the danger.

As the final whistle went, the crowd rose to acclaim the performances of both teams in the 25–25 result – the highest scoring draw in international rugby.

Kenneth Grant MacLeod, early 1900s

Perhaps the most talented all-rounder from the early days of the 20th century was Kenneth Grant MacLeod.

MacLeod was a 15-year-old pupil at Fettes College in Edinburgh when the Scottish selectors wanted him for international duty, but his headmaster would have none of it. However, at the age of 17 years 9 months and by then at Cambridge University, he picked up his first cap against Dave Gallagher's All-Blacks at Inverleith in 1905.

Further caps followed at centre, in tandem with his brother Lewis, and also at wing, most notably against Paul Roo's Springboks at Hampden Park in November 1906, when MacLeod scored one of the best Scotland tries ever. After ten caps in total, though, he retired. His two older brothers had been seriously injured playing rugby and his father was keen for him to take up another sport.

And this MacLeod duly did. At Cambridge, he had become a 'triple' blue, in rugby, cricket and athletics, also winning the Scottish Long Jump Championship in 1906, but cricket was the sport to which he next turned his prodigious talents.

MacLeod played for Lancashire in the years before the First World War, making his name as an all-rounder with a penchant for big-hitting. An appearance for the Gentlemen against the Players in 1909, the occasional first-class hockey match, plus rumours of several trials for Manchester City were also included on his CV.

When war started, MacLeod became a captain in the 3rd Gordons and served in France, where he was gassed and also mentioned in dispatches. Afterwards, he lived in Strathspey for a time, gaining a reputation in the hunting-and-shooting field, before emigrating to South Africa, where he won the Natal Seniors Golf Championship before mellowing to star at contract bridge. He died in Cape Town at the age of 79 in 1967.

Nil: 0–0 draws in rugby

No score draws in rugby are, thankfully, a comparative rarity. In fact, in a statistical list of Scotland's internationals which began with an encounter against England in 1871, Scotland has been involved in only 11 , as listed here:

v England

8 March	1875	Raeburn Place
4 March	1878	Kennington Oval
8 March	1883	Hamilton Crescent
13 March	1886	Raeburn Place
10 March	1900	Inverleith
15 March	1930	Twickenham

v Wales

19 January	1885	Hamilton Crescent

v Ireland

18 February	1893	Ballynafeigh, Belfast
15 February	1896	Lansdowne Road
24 February	1900	Lansdowne Road

v New Zealand

18 January	1964	Murrayfield

On the blind side, 1920

When Scotland met France on 1 January 1920 at Parc des Princes in the first international after the end of the First World War, three players each of whom had lost an eye during the war took the field, including 'Jock' Wemyss of Edinburgh Wanderers.

One hundred and eleven line–outs, 1963

When Wales won 6–0 at Murrayfield on 2 February 1963, it came after four consecutive defeats in Scotland. The Welsh captain, fly-half Rowlands, realising his pack was two stone a man heavier than the home side, decided on keeping the play tight, almost ignoring his backs.

At every opportunity, he punted the ball into touch, with the result that there were a record 111 line-outs during the game.

One player – two countries, James March

In 1889, Scotland played only two rugby internationals, one against Wales and the other against Ireland, as relations with England were still in dispute after a disputd try. For both games, which Scotland won, James Marsh, from Edinburgh Institute FPs, played a notable part in the three-quarter line. By that time, Marsh had also qualified in medicine from Edinburgh University.

Three years later, at Manchester, that same James Marsh was in the England team which beat Ireland 7–0. Marsh had moved to general practice in the Manchester area and joined Swinton Rugby Club where his strong play caught the eye of the England selectors. They named him at centre for the annual North versus South match in 1891, and the following season he won his one and only cap for England.

James Marsh remains the only man ever to have played for two Unions in the International Championship.

Quick rugger man: John Leslie

In 1923, at Twickenham, hero Leo Price touched down for England against Wales after only 10 seconds. That record lasted for 76 years, until Scotland lined up against Wales at Murrayfield in February 1999, in the last Five Nations Championship.

Stand-off Duncan Hodge lined-up as if to take an orthodox kick towards his forwards to the right. As the referee blew his whistle to start the match, Hodge switched direction and kicked left, where there were fewer Welsh players. None of them, though, matched the anticipation and reaction of the Scottish inside-centre John Leslie, who swooped for the ball, snatched it out of the grasp of two Welsh players, raced for the line and touched the ball down to the left of the posts.

The crowd was amazed, and delighted; at least those in their seats were. Many others were still making their way to their positions when the roar went up. 'How long had it taken?' everyone was asking. The

BBC broadcasters were ready to check the re-run, which showed that John Leslie had scored in nine seconds, setting a new world record for an international match. Could that ever be beaten?

Relatives capped for Scotland at rugby, 1871–2000

Father and Son

> J.B. Waters (1904); F.H. Waters (1930)
>
> H.T.S. Gedge (1894); P.M.S. Gedge (1933)
>
> J.H. Bruce Lockhart (1913); R.B. Bruce Lockhart (1937); L. Bruce Lockhart (1948)
>
> R.A. Gallie (1920); G.H. Gallie (1939)
>
> I.C. Geddes (1906); K.I. Geddes (1947)
>
> A.T. Sloan (1914); D.A. Sloan (1950)
>
> H. Waddell (1924); G.H. Waddell (1957)
>
> W.M. Simmers (1927); B.M. Simmers (1965)
>
> A.T. Fisher (1947); C.D. Fisher (1975)
>
> J.J. Hegarty (1951); C.B. Hegarty (1978)
>
> M.J. Campbell-Lamerton (1961); J.R.E. Campbell-Lamerton (1986)

Brothers

> G.T. Neilson (1891); W. Neilson (1891); W.G. Neilson (1894); R.T Neilson (1898)
>
> J.F. Finlay (1871); A.B. Finlay (1875); N.J. Finlay (1875)
>
> J.W. Arthur (1871); A. Arthur (1875)
>
> W. Cross (1871); M. Cross (1875)
>
> R.W. Irvine (1871); D.R. Irvine (1878)
>
> T.R. Marshall (1871); W. Marshall (1872)
>
> J.H. McClure (1872); G.B. McClure (1873)
>
> J. Reid (1874); C. Reid (1881)
>
> R. Ainslie (1879); T. Ainslie (1881)
>
> R. Maitland (1881); G. Maitland (1885)
>
> A. Walker (1881); J.G. Walker (1882)
>
> A.R. Don Wauchope (1881); P.H. Don Wauchope (1885)
>
> M.C. McEwan (1886); W.M.C. McEwan (1894)

C.E. Orr (1887); J.E. Orr (1889)

J.H. Dods (1895); F.P. Dods (1901)

D.R. Bedell-Sivright (1900); J.V. Bedell-Sivright (1902)

J.E. Crabbie (1900); G.E. Crabbie (1904)

J. Ross (1901); E.J. Ross (1904)

L.M. MacLeod (1904); K.G. MacLeod (1905)

A.B.H.L. Purves (1906); W.D.C.L. Purves (1912)

D.G. McGregor (1907); J.R. McGregor (1909)

C.D. Stuart (1909); L.M. Stuart (1923)

J.D. Dobson (1901); J. Dobson (1911)

D.D. Howie (1912); R.A. Howie (1924)

G.M. Murray (1921); R.O. Murray (1935)

J.C. Dykes (1922); A.S Dykes (1932)

J.M. Henderson (1933); I.C. Henderson (1939)

R.W. Shaw (1934); I. Shaw (1937)

R.B. Bruce Lockhart (1937); L. Bruce Lockhart (1948)

T.F. Dorward (1928); A.F. Dorward (1950)

D.D. Valentine (1947); A.R. Valentine (1953)

A. Cameron (1948); D. Cameron (1953)

R.W.T. Chisholm (1955); D.H. Chisholm (1964)

C. Elliot (1958); T.G. Elliot (1968)

T.O. Grant (1960); D. Grant (1965)

A.C.W. Boyle (1963); A.H.W. Boyle (1966)

P.C. Brown (1964); G.L. Brown (1969)

B.M. Gossman (1980); J.S. Gossman (1980)

I.G. Milne (1979); K.S. Milne (1989); D.F. Milne (1991)

J.H. Calder (1981); F. Calder (1986)

A.G. Hastings (1986); S. Hastings (1986)

P.W. Dods (1983); M. Dods (1994)

J. Leslie (1998); M. Leslie (1998)

G. Bulloch (1997); A. Bulloch (2000)

Grandfather and Grandson

G.F. Ritchie (1932); A.D. Nicol (1992)

J.M. Bannerman (1921); D.S. Munro (1994)

Rugby at Hampden? 1896, 1906

Hampden has been the venue for two Scottish rugby internationals. In 1896, Old Hampden Park was the venue for Scotland's final match of the season (France had not yet joined the Championship). A 6–0 defeat at Cardiff in January had been followed by a 0–0 draw with Ireland at Lansdowne Road. So the goodly crowd which turned up at this unusual venue for the match on 14 March against England was not expecting too much.

However, the Scots rose to the occasion. The pack dominated the play and gave the aggressive backs a good supply of ball. Right-wing H.T.S. Hodge (London Scottish), left wing J.J. Cowans (London Scottish) and centre C.J.N Fleming (Watsonians) all scored tries, with T.M. Scott (Hawick) converting one of the three, for an 11–0 win.

Ten years later, on 17 November 1906, a crowd of 32,000 was at Hampden Park to see Scotland take on the visiting South Africans. Two days of heavy rain made the ground sodden and heavy, conditions not suited to South Africans' running style but ideally suited for the hard-working Scots pack.

By half-time, there had been no score. Shortly after the re-start, scrum-half P. Munro broke away to his left from a scrum at the centre, and when confronted by the defence he hoisted a high kick across the field to the right wing where K.G. McLeod (Cambridge U), running at full speed, caught the ball cleanly and ran away from the defence along the touchline to score at the corner.

Shortly afterwards, a good forward rush by the Scots gave left-winger Purves (London Scottish) the chance to increase the lead to 6–0, and that remained the score at the final whistle.

Rugby records, 1882–1990

International Championship

This began in 1882. It has usually included the four home nations and also France from 1910–31, then again from 1947 onwards. Scotland has won it outright on 14 occasions: 1887, 1891, 1895, 1901, 1903, 1904, 1907, 1925, 1929, 1933, 1938, 1984, 1990 & 1999.

Scotland has also shared the championship 8 times: with England, 1886, 1890; with Ireland, 1926, 1927; with Wales, 1964; with France, 1986; with England and Wales, 1920. Quintuple tie, 1973.

Until 1992, there was no trophy available for the winner of the championship. In 1993, however, a very handsome cup, the 'Five Nations' Championship Trophy', was presented for the competition. The first names on it were France, in 1993, and Wales, in 1994. In 1999, the name of Scotland made a first appearance.

And from 2000, of course, with the inclusion of Italy, the name has been changed to the 'Six Nations Championship Trophy'.

The Triple Crown

It has been suggested that this mythical award was coined by newspaper reporters in the late 19th century. To win it, a home country must beat the other three home nations in any one international season.

To date, Scotland has won the Triple Crown on 10 occasions; 1891, 1895, 1901, 1903, 1907, 1925, 1933, 1938, 1984, & 1990.

Most tries in one match

Scotland scored a record 12 tries against Wales in February 1887. This tally was matched by Wales v France in 1910 and England v France in 1914.

Tries in all four games

A.C. Wallace of Scotland is one of four players to have achieved this feat, when he played for the Grand Slam team of 1925. The others are H.C. Catcheside (England) 1924; P. Esteve (France) 1983; and P. Sella (France) 1986.

Most tries in one match

G.C. Lindsay (Scotland) 1887.

Most tries in a single championship

I.S. Smith (Scotland) 1925.

Scotland's World Cup record, 1987–2003

The inaugural competition for the Webb Ellis Trophy took place in 1987 in Australia and New Zealand:

Scotland 20 France 20; Scotland 60 Zimbabwe 21; Scotland 55 Romania 28

QF Scotland 3 New Zealand 30

1991, England, Ireland, Scotland and Wales: Scotland 47 Japan 9; Scotland 51 Zimbabwe 12; Scotland 24 Ireland 15

QF Scotland 28 Western Samoa 6

SF Scotland 6 England 9

3rd–4th place play-off: Scotland 6 New Zealand 13

1995, South Africa: Scotland 89 Ivory Coast 0; Scotland 41 Tonga 5; Scotland 19 France 22

QF Scotland 30 New Zealand 48

1999, Great Britain: Scotland 29 South Africa 46; Scotland 43; Uruguay 12; Scotland 48 Spain 0

QF play-off: Scotland 35 Samoa 20

QF: Scotland 18 New Zealand 30

2003, Australia: Scotland 22 Japan 11; Scotland 32 USA 15; Scotland 22 Fiji 20

QF: Scotland 16 Australia 33.

Scots miss out on the All Blacks

In the early days of the twentieth century, the SRU was a very conservative organisation. They were always keen to maintain a pure amateurism in the real world, and, occasionally, they overdid it. When Jock Weymss played for Scotland after the First World War (in which he had lost an eye) he was charged seven shillings and sixpence (37½p) for a jersey it was claimed he had not returned after a pre-war international.

When the New Zealand national team toured Britain in 1905 their Union made daily expense payments to players. The SRU criticised the New Zealand Union for doing so and a rift developed between the unions, which lasted nearly thirty years. Relations were so bad that the touring All Blacks in 1924–25 did not play in Scotland and rugby fans were denied the chance of seeing the team dubbed 'The Invincibles' who won all 28 matches in their tour of the rest of the British Isles.

A Scots referee upsets the All Blacks, 1905

The 1905 All Blacks had cut a successful swathe through England and Scotland, beating the latter 12–7 at Inverleith. The Welsh, though, were reigning champions and Triple Crown holders, so their clash with the visitors in December 1905 was eagerly anticipated.

An estimated 40,000 crammed into the old wooden stands and enclosures of Cardiff Arms Park. The gates were closed long before kick-off, the New Zealanders performed their traditional Haka, the Welsh players and crowd responded with 'Land of My Fathers'. The atmosphere was electric.

The first-half play was equally good, Wales probably having the better of it and going in at the interval 3–0 up. Stung by this reverse, a very determined All Blacks side raced out for the second half. Time after time, they attacked the Welsh line; each time, the Welsh kept them out. Near the end, though, came the incident which caused all the controversy.

Centre Bob Dean went full tilt for the line and attempted to ground the ball. Many thought that he had done so but the referee, John Dallas, of Scotland, decided that Deans had been held up in the tackle and said 'no try': Shortly afterwards, he blew the whistle and the crowd went wild with delight, cheering their heroes as the defeated All Blacks sadly left the field.

Unfortunately for Dallas, the controversy continued. The *Daily Mail* gave the match a full review and their reporter was quite clear on the incident, 'Deans was collared but not before he had crossed the Welsh line ... some of the Welsh players admit that the equalizing try was actually scored and that Deans, after crossing the line was pulled back.'

The controversy continued for years. John Dallas continued to insist that Deans had not scored; the Welsh believed he was right; many neutrals were in two minds. And whenever New Zealanders visited Cardiff, one of the highlights was a trip to Cardiff Arms Park to view the scene of the incident.

Second Grand Slam, 1984

After the first Grand Slam win of 1925, Scots rugby fans had a long wait for the second. Yet it came at a rather unusual time, after some poor seasons. In the early 1980s Scotland finished third in the Five Nations Championship in 1980–81 and 1981–82; and fourth in 1982–83.

A defeat by the touring Barbarians in March 1983 hardly lifted morale, although the 25–25 draw with New Zealand in November gave the fans a boost. Still, as they travelled to Cardiff for the first match of the 1983–84 season, the fans were realistic rather than confident. However, the Scottish forwards proved to be a revelation and set the groundmark for a fine victory, although the lack of inspiration among the backs was a continuing worry.

21 January 1984: Wales 9, Scotland 15; tries: I. Paxton, J. Aitken; conversions: P. Dods (2); penalties, P. Dods.

England were next up, at Murrayfield, the hundredth international between the two countries. The visitors concentrated on the use of set pieces but the Scots buzzed about in the loose, again giving plenty of ball to the backs, who scored two tries, the rest of the points coming from kicks.

4 February 1984: Scotland 18, England 6; tries: D. Johnston, A. Kennedy; conversions, P. Dods (2); penalties, P, Dods (2).

A trip to Lansdowne Road can be a tricky experience for any side, but this time round the Scottish tails were up and they never let Ireland into the game. Surprisingly, the home side, having won the toss, elected to play into the wind and the Scots made them suffer, scoring 12 points in the first 14 minutes and 22 in the first half. Ireland did raise their game after the interval but could not hold back the Tartan tide. This was Scotlands first Triple Crown since 1938.

3 March 1984: Ireland 9, Scotland 32; tries: R. Laidlaw (2); K. Robertson, P. Dods; conversions, P, Dods (3); penalties, P. Dods (2); one penalty try.

And that set up a finale against France at Murrayfield. The Scots had to cope with intense French pressure in the first quarter of the game but they managed to weather the storm and turned the game round in the second half.

With the score at 12–9 in favour of France, the visitors were penalised for an indiscretion 50 metres from their own goal. The distance was a trifle too far even for a kicker of Peter Dods's ability. Unfortunately for the French, though, their indiscipline spilled over into an argument with the referee, who ordered them back 10 metres and made the kick a possibility. Peter Dods made no mistake to even the scores, and from then on it was Scotland's day. A second Grand Slam had been achieved. Peter Dods' 17 points equalled the record held by Andy Irvine; and his 50 points for a season was a new Scottish record.

19 March 1984: Scotland 21, France 12; tries, J. Calder; conversions, P. Dodds; penalties, P. Dodds (5).

	P	W	D	L	F	A	Pts
Scotland	4	4	0	0	86	36	8
France	4	3	0	1	90	67	6
Wales	4	2	0	2	67	60	4
England	4	1	0	3	51	83	2
Ireland	4	0	0	4	39	87	0

The Barbarians arrive, 1970

Scotland 17 Barbarians 33, 9 May 1970

This was the Barbarians' first-ever visit to Murrayfield and they comfortably beat a Scots team just about to set out on a tour of Australia.

The Scots were severely handicapped when they lost right-winger Mike Smith to injury after only three minutes; and they also played the last fifteen without scrum-half Dunky Paterson. However, although the home side won a lot of ball at the line-outs, they could not cope with the Barbarians' attacking flair, which resulted in seven tries.

The Calcutta Cup

British émigrés in Calcutta in the 1870s used polo and tennis as outlets for their sporting energies but there were some rugby men pining for their favourite sport.

Some of these wrote letters to the *Englishmen* and the *Indian Daily News* to try to drum up interest, and this campaign eventually bore fruit. On Christmas Day 1872, a match was played between a team of 20 players representing England and a combined 20 representing Scotland, Ireland and Wales. The match was such a success that a repeat was played out a week later!

Calcutta Football Club was founded in 1873. One year later, the club was admitted to the Rugby Football Union. Unfortunately, although the club was very solvent financially, lack of opposition proved a major problem, and after four years the Calcutta Club folded. The question then arose of what to do with the club funds. After one or two 'fun' suggestions, the Club Captain, G.A. James Rothney, suggested the purchasing of a trophy of outstanding Indian craftsmanship, and that this should be offered to the RFU in London. On 20 December 1877, he sent a letter to the RFU to that effect, their intention being . . . 'The best means of doing some lasting good for the case of Rugby Football and as a slight memento of the Calcutta Club . . .'

The RFU's response was very positive and they accepted the offer as an . . . 'international challenge cup to be played for annually between England and Scotland, the cup remaining the property of the Rugby Football Union'.

The Calcutta Club officials then closed the bank account, withdrew the money in silver rupees and had these melted down and worked by the finest Indian craftsmen into an elegant trophy, 18 inches high, with the handles in the form of cobras and the lid surmounted by an elephant.

The first Calcutta Cup match was played at Raeburn Place, Edinburgh on 10 March 1897 and ended in a draw. All in, up to the end of season 2004–05, the two countries have met on 122 occasions, with England winning 64 times, Scotland 40 and 17 drawn.

Third Grand Slam, 1990

After waiting 39 years between the First Grand Slam (1925) and the Second (1984), followers of Scottish rugby were not expecting another for some time. Yet, to the surprise of many, and the utter astonishment of the English, it came to pass in 1990.

A 32–0 win over Romania in December 1989 gave the whole of Scottish rugby a boost, and it was with some confidence that team and support travelled to Dublin two months later. This turned out to be an error-strewn match with Scotland winning despite missing goal-kicks and try-scoring opportunities. They also came off second best in the line-outs but the forwards put in some great work in the loose.

3 February 1990: Ireland 10 Scotland 13; try, D. White (2); conversions, C. Chalmers; penalties, C. Chalmers.

Scotland's next fixture was at home to France and they had every reason to be confident about this one, as France had lost their five previous matches at Murrayfield. The Scots had the advantage of a strong wind in the first-half but went in only 3–0 ahead. Sadly, for the French, the wind dropped in the second-half, they lost a forward to injury and the great full-back Serge Blanco had a day he will not want to remember.

17 February 1990: Scotland 21 France 0; tries: F. Calder, I. Tukalo; conversions, C. Chalmers (2); penalties, C. Chalmers (2), G. Hastings (1).

The Neath club provided seven players plus the coach for the next match against Scotland in Cardiff, yet this turned out to be a poor Welsh team. Scotland dominated the game, and although the home side hammered away, they lacked the invention to pierce a strong Scottish defence. At the end though, there were only a few points in it.

3 March 1990: Wales 9 Scotland 13; try, D. Cronin; penalties, C. Chalmers (3).

With a Calcutta Cup, a Triple Crown, a Grand Slam and a Five Nations at stake, the Scotland–England clash was hyped to the heavens. It was thought that the Scots would come out at 100 mph to show their determination, but David Sole led out them out to the Murrayfield pitch with slow, determined steps. The crowd caught the mood and did their bit: never has 'Flower of Scotland' been sung with such volume and flavour. The English were favourites: a draw would be enough to give them the Championship. But the Scots took command from the start, rattled the visitors with their drive and enthusiasm, and took advantage of two penalties to go 6–0 ahead. However, a great try by Jeremy Guscott – England's first at Murrayfield in 10 years – pulled it back to 6–4 before another penalty for Scotland made it 9–4 at the interval.

In the first minute of the second-half came the crucial score. Gary Armstrong gave the ball to Gavin Hastings, who, just before he was pushed into touch, managed a high kick ahead. The English defence got caught flat-footed as Tony Stanger and Finlay Calder raced after the ball, the winger using his height to reach for it and get the touch. The conversion was missed and the English came at the Scots like demons. They kept the pressure on but the Scots, urged by the crowd, held for a famous victory.

The Calcutta Cup, a Triple Crown, a Grand Slam and the Five Nations Championship all belonged to Scotland.

17 March 1990: Scotland 13 England 9; try, T. Stanger; penalties, C. Chalmers (3).

	P	W	D	L	F	A	Pts
Scotland	4	4	0	0	60	26	8
England	4	3	0	1	90	26	6
France	4	2	0	2	67	78	4
Ireland	4	1	0	2	36	75	2
France	4	0	0	4	42	90	0

Trouble: Scotland v Wales, 1921

When Scotland beat Wales at Swansea on 5 February 1921, by 14 points to 8, it was the first win in the principality since 1892.

However, the match was equally remarkable for the unprecedented crowd scenes, play having to be held up several times to move the spectators from the touchlines and goal areas. At one time, the referee, Mr Baxter, from England, conferred with the two captains about abandoning the game: and when Scotland's right-winger scored the winning try, he put the ball down amongst many spectators sitting in the Welsh goal area.

Even after the match, the Scots' day was not finished. Due to the interruptions, the players had to grab their clothes from the dressing-room, rush onto the bus, and race for the station to catch their train home. Only on the train did they have time to wash and change.

Twenty–a–side to fifteen–a–side, 1877

In the early days, Scottish rugby teams were made up of 20 players, roughly laid out as 4 full-backs, 4 half-backs and 12 forwards.

Quite a few teams had switched to 15-a-side by the 1860s, yet when the 1870 challenge to English clubs was issued the figure of players suggested was 20, a number which was accepted and maintained for a number of years. However, after a committee meeting in December 1875, the Scottish Football Union wrote to its English counterpart suggesting a change to 15s but the RFU decided it was too late in the season to accept the alteration.

The SFU repeated the suggestion after an AGM in October 1876 and this time the RFU agreed, with the result that the England–Ireland match at the Oval in February 1877 was the first international played with 15 players on each side.

Scotland's first with 15 players was also against Ireland at Ormeau, Belfast, on 19 February 1877. In rain which fell throughout the match Scotland won by 4 goals, 2 drop-goals and 2 tries to nil.

Under water: New Zealand v Scotland, 1975

The international between New Zealand and Scotland at Auckland on 14 June 1975 should never have taken place.

Something like four inches of rain had fallen in less than twelve hours and large areas of the field were under water. But the organisers had little choice. The Scots were flying home the following day, so no alternative date was possible, and around £85,000 had been taken in from 55,000 spectators in pre-match sales. That would have been handed back in the event of a cancellation.

The match went ahead in appalling conditions, with around 45,000 in the stadium. Scotland faced torrential rain in the first half. At the interval, the wind changed direction, so in the second half they faced the same conditions once more. Perhaps it was not surprising that they lost 24–0.

Two after-match comments reflected the feelings of the teams. The New Zealand captain delivered that it was 'one of the greatest moments in New Zealand swimming'. And a Scots prop remarked, 'It was sheer luck that nobody drowned.'

Unusual rugby moments: 1879–1925

First match for the Calcutta Cup
Raeburn Place, Edinburgh, 10 March 1879
Scotland 1 drop-goal   England 1 goal   Match drawn
Record crowd of 10,000

First match played on a Saturday
Hamilton Crescent, Glasgow, 14 February 1880
Scotland 1 goal, 2 dropped goals, 2 tries   Ireland 0

Tom Anderson
Tom Anderson, still at Merchiston School and 19 years of age, was at full-back when Scotland beat Ireland by two tries to nil on 18 February 1882 at Hamilton Crescent in Glasgow. In September of that same year, Anderson was capped for a Scottish Cricket XI against the touring Australians.

The first time a neutral official was used
Whalley Range, Manchester, 4 March 1882
England 0   Scotland 2 tries
Referee: Mr Robinson (Ireland)

Abandoned
Ormeau, Belfast, 21 February 1885
Ireland 0   Scotland 1 try

This match was played on a waterlogged pitch, with gale-force winds blasting sleet across it. No sensible football was possible and by mutual consent the game was abandoned after 20 minutes. In the evening, it was agreed that this would stand as a win for Scotland unless the Irish played a second match in Edinburgh. This they did on 7 March 1886 Raeburn Place, Edinburgh.

Scotland 1 goal, 2 tries   Ireland nil

Mounted police on show
Raeburn Place, Edinburgh, 13 March 1886
Scotland nil   England nil
For the first time ever, a police force of 36 constables was reinforced by mounted police.

Caps
In season 1891–92, for the first time, the Union committee agreed that trophy caps would be awarded by the Union, instead of the players having to buy them.

Hampden
The first match played at football's national stadium took place on 14 March 1886, when Scotland beat England 11–0.

First match against foreign opposition
Inverleith, Edinburgh, 18 November 1905
Scotland 7   New Zealand 12

First fixture against French opposition
April 1896, Edinburgh, XV v Paris XV, Paris
In 1898, a French XV played one match at Myreside and one at Hamilton Crescent.

First match versus France at full level
Inverleith, Edinburgh, 22 January 1910
Scotland 27   France 0

Last match against France before the split
Murrayfield, 24 January 1931
Scotland 6   France 4

First match after the split
Colombes Stadium, 1 January 1947
France 8   Scotland 3

Last international at Inverleith
24 January 1925   Scotland 25   France 4

Numbered jerseys
After the First World War, when other countries started to number their players, the SRU had reservations. When King George V, at Twickenham in 1924, inquired of the Scottish Rugby Union President why the Scots players were nor numbered, he received a brusque reply, 'This is a rugby match, not a cattle market!'

Victory Internationals, 1946

In the first season after the Second World War, Scotland played a series of six 'Victory' internationals against the other home nations and one Army side. Results were as follows:

19 January	1946	Scotland 11	New Zealand Army 6	Murrayfield
2 February	1946	Scotland 25	Wales 6	Swansea
23 February	1946	Scotland 9	Ireland 0	Murrayfield
16 March	1946	Scotland 8	England 12	Twickenham
30 March	1946	Scotland 13	Wales 11	Murrayfield
13 April	1946	Scotland 27	England 0	Murrayfield

Wartime internationals

The Calcutta Cup match of 21 March 1914 marked the end of an epoch. It was the last match played before the conflict began.

Before the end of 1914, three of the thirty players on the pitch were gone and by 1918, five of the English and six of the Scottish XV had been killed in action.

Scotland's first match after the war was against France, at the Parc des Princes, on 1 January 1920.

Another Calcutta Cup match on 18 March 1939, ended the official international action before the Second World War. The first official match for Scotland after the war was again in Paris, this time at the Colombes Stadium.

However, between 1942 and 1945, a series of matches were played involving servicemen from Scotland and England. The results were as follows:

21 March	1942	Scotland 21 England 6	Inverleith
11 April	1942	Scotland 8 England 5	Wembley
27 February	1943	Scotland 6 England 29	Inverleith
10 April	1943	Scotland 19 England 24	Leicester
26 February	1944	Scotland 13 England 23	Murrayfield
18 March	1944	Scotland 15 England 27	Leicester
24 February	1945	Scotland 18 England 11	Leicester
17 March	1945	Scotland 5 England 16	Murrayfield

When a referee forgot

At Murrayfield, in January 1976, Scotland were 3–0 up against France thanks to a drop-goal by scrum-half Dougie Morgan. After that, the match became a battle of the kicks as both sides tried to cope in the windswept conditions. Andy Irvine missed one and then had another attempt which he sent high over the bar to put Scotland 6–0 up. The referee, however, refused to allow the kick.

Into the high wind, Irvine had asked for the ball to be steadied. Ian McLaughlin took on the task and, with Irvine being a round-the-corner kicker, lay in front of the ball to hold it. The referee, Ken Pattinson of England, declared that this put him offside at the time of the kick and ordered a scrum. Unfortunately, that was a mistake. The laws of the game at that time clearly stated that the ball-holder could be in front of the kicker.

Scotland eventually went down 6–13 to France and arguments raged for weeks over the referee's decisions. Mr Pattinson was big enough to admit his mistake: but he never again took control of an international match.

Young caps in rugby, 1870s–1900s

Rugby always gets the reputation of being a man's game, yet Scotland, in particular, has capped a number of extremely young players.

Curiously, two of them were the same age – 17 years 36 days – when they first pulled on the dark blue jersey. A back, Ninian Findlay (Edinburgh Academy), was selected to play against England in 1875. His nine-match international career ended in 1881, but on his second last game, against Ireland, a new team-mate was Charles 'Hippo' Reid (Edinburgh Academy), also the same age when he ran out in that match.

Others capped while under 18 included the following:

		Born	*Age*
W.G. Nielson	Merchiston	31.1.1876	17 years 5 months
W. Neilson	Merchiston	18.8.1873	17 years 5 months
K.G. MacLeod	Fettes	02.02.1888	17 years 9 months
L.M. Balfour	Edinburgh Acadamey	09.03.1854	17 years 10 months
A. Arthur	Glasgow Acadamey	03.04.1857	17 years 11 months
R.W. Irvine	Edinburgh Acadamey	19.04.1871	17 years 11 months

As mentioned elsewhere, K.G. MacLeod was capped for the first time against New Zealand in 1905 but he had been chosen in 1903 at the age of 15, only for his headmaster at Fettes College to refuse permission.

SAILING

A talented trooper: Chay Blyth, 1960s

Originally from Hawick, Chay Blyth joined the paratroopers in the early 1960s, becoming the youngest sergeant since the Second World War. In 1966, he and Captain John Ridgeway became the first men to row across the Atlantic in an open boat, a 20-feet dory. After completing this feat in 92 days, Blyth was awarded the British Empire Medal.

Five years later, Blyth was the first person to sail westwards around the world against the prevailing wind and currents. His record – in the ketch *British Steel* – lasted for 23 years. This feat gained him the title of Yachtsman of the Year, the Chichester Trophy and a CBE.

Since then, Chay Blyth has collected a whole list of racing successes, including:

1973–74	In the yacht *Great Britain*, with a crew of paratroopers, he took honours in the Whitbread Round the World Yacht Race.
1978	In the yacht *Great Britain IV* won the Round Britain Race.
1981	In the yacht *Brittany Ferries* C.B. won the Two-Handed Trans-Alantic Race with companion Rob James, breaking the existing record.
1982	In the yacht *Brittany Ferries* came second overall, first in Class 1 Round Britain and Ireland Race.
1983	In the trimaran *Beefeater II*, with companion Eric Blunn, capsized off Cape Horn during New York–San Francisco record attempt and spent 19 hours in water before being rescued.
1986	Co-Skipper on the successful Blue Riband – *Virgin Atlantic Challenger II*.
1989	Founded Challenge Business to organise the British Steel Challenge. This event allowed ordinary people to sail around the world in a professionally organised race.
1996	The success of British Steel Challenge led to an even more successful BT Global Challenge 1996–97. BT sponsored the event again in 2000–01.
1997	Chay Blyth was knighted for his services to sailing. He also received an honorary Doctorate of Law from the University of Portsmouth.

The Flying Dutchman Scot: Rodney Pattison, 1968–76

Rodney Pattison won two Olympic gold medals and one silver medal in the Flying Dutchman class – a 2-man, 20ft-long dinghy.

At the Mexico Olympics in 1968 he won his first gold, partnered by Ian McDonald Smith, winning five out of six races, finishing second once and incurring only three penalty points to record the lowest ever score in an Olympic regatta. In 1972, at Munich, with Christopher Davies, he won another gold medal: the silver came with Julian Brooke Haughton in 1976 in Montreal.

SNOOKER

Scots stars on the green baize: Stephen Hendry

Scottish Professional Champion at 17 years of age, Auchterarder-born Stephen Hendry dominated the world of snooker in the 1990s even more than Steve Davis did in the previous decade.

World Champion at 21, he went on to win the title another six times, making seven in total. Hendry has won over 30 ranking tournaments and his career is continuing.

In 1998, John Higgins, from Lanarkshire, won his first World Title.

The first 148

In the history of snooker, there have been relatively few breaks of 147. Indeed, in competitive play, only 49 'maximums' have ever been recorded. On Sunday, 17 October 2004, however, a Scot improved on that figure, when Jamie Burnett made a break of 148.

The usual way of compiling a 147 is for the player to pot 15 reds followed by 15 blacks, then go through the colours: yellow, green, brown, blue, pink and black. But Burnett made his total by a different route.

He started by taking the brown as a free ball, then followed this up with the brown as a colour. That made 5.

He moved on to take 15 reds, along with 12 blacks, 2 pinks and a blue. That all moved him on to 121. And Burnett then cleared all the colours, bringing his total to 148.

That gives him a place in the record books but unfortunately, as the break came in a qualifying round, there was no corresponding financial reward for his new record.

The first 147 Scot: John Rea, 1989

The first ever officially ratified snooker break of 147 was by Joe Davis of England in the Leicester Square Hall in London on 22 January 1955.

It took some time for a Scot to get to the same standard. In fact, we had to wait until 18 February 1989 when John Rea completed the maximum break at Marco's Leisure Centre in Glasgow.

Walter Donaldson, 1920s–50s

Born in Coatbridge, Lanarkshire, in 1907, Walter Donaldson was the first Scottish-born player to make his name in the world of snooker.

Walter won the national under-16 billiards championships in 1922 and turned professional the following year. He did not enter the World Snooker Championship until 1933 when he lost in the semi-finals to Joe Davis. He missed the next five championships, but came back in 1939, when he reached the quarter-finals, and in 1940, when he went out at the semi-final stage.

After war service in the Army, Walter resumed his snooker career. With the retirement of Joe Davis, he vied with Fred Davis for the number one position. He reached eight consecutive world finals from 1947 to 1954, beating Fred Davis in the first of these to take the title.

Fred won the next two but Walter beat him in 1950 to take his second championship. He then became disillusioned with the sport and retired, turning his snooker room into a cow-shed and using the slats from his table to make crazy-paving for a patio!

Walter Donaldson died at his home in Buckinghamshire in 1973.

UK Under 16s Billiards Champion	1922
World Professional Snooker Champion	1947 & 1950
World Professional Snooker Runner-up	1948, 1949, 1951, 1952, 1953 & 1954.

Water stops play – in snooker, 1999

In the 1999 World Snooker Championships, held as usual at the Crucible Theatre in Sheffield, the semi-final encounter between Scotland's John Higgins and Mark William's of Wales was held up when water dripped on to the table.

Investigations showed that water had built-up on an overhead TV gantry and eventually spilled down on to the baize surface. It certainly stopped play for a while. When it resumed, Williams went on to win the match, but lost out to another Scot, Stephen Hendry, in the final.

SWIMMING

A tragic early demise: Nancy Riach

Nancy Riach, a member of Motherwell Amateur Swimming and Water Polo Club, was regarded as the finest swimmer in the British Empire, and by 1945, at the age of 18, held 28 Scottish and British records.

In 1946 she was British champion at 100, 220 and 440 yards freestyle distances. However, after one of her races at the European Swimming Championships in 1947 she contracted polio, which cost her her life. She was 20 years of age.

No 50-metre pool: Bobby McGregor

Bobby McGregor grew up with swimming in his blood, his father David having been in the GB water-polo team for the 1936 Olympics. Based in Falkirk, McGregor won six British sprint titles: silver medals in the 1962 and 1966 Commonwealth Games and a gold in the 1966 European Championships.

In the 1964 Olympics, McGregor held the lead in the closing stages of the 100 metres, only to be overtaken in the last 5 metres by the American, Don Schollander, who won by 1/10 second – about 6 inches.

Quite a career. And all this at a time when Scotland did not have a 50-metre pool!

Off the high board: Peter Heatley

Peter Heatley dominated Scottish swimming for 21 years, besides representing Scotland and Great Britain round the world.

A self-taught diver, Heatley was East of Scotland Champion from 1937–39 and Scottish Swimming Champion from 1946–58. He also held the Scottish freestyle titles between 1942 and 1946.

At international level, Heatley won Commonwealth gold medals for highboard in 1950 and 1958, plus the springboard in 1954.

Portobello outdoor swimming pool

Ten thousand people were present for the opening of the pool in 1936 when Lord Provost Louis S. Gumley did the honours.

Unfortunately, the weather was showery, but later on bouts of sunshine broke through to reward the spectators. The pool was the biggest in Europe and could seat 6,000. It also had the added attraction of a wave machine. When that was first set in motion at the opening, there was much laughter as the foamy breakers crashed on to the 'beach', with those closest being showered by spray.

A full programme of events followed the opening. A swimming display by a team from Renfrew School was followed by a thrilling demonstration of diving by, among others, T.J. Maher, the British High Diving Champion, and Miss Cecily Cousins, the National Ladies' High Diving Champion.

N.B. Despite much opposition from the general public and a personal plea from Sean Connery – a former lifeguard at the pool – the Portobello Pool was closed and demolished in 1988.

The hardest way to cross the channel

One can cross the English Channel, or *La Manche*, to use its French title, in a variety of ways, but surely swimming across is the most difficult and exhausting.

On 24 August 1875, Captain Matthew Webb dived off the end of Admiralty Pier at Dover and went on to complete the first unaided swim across the English Channel. Thirty-six years would pass before anyone matched his feat.

Many tried, though. One of the most persistent was a native of Glasgow, Jabez Wolffe, who between 1906 and 1913 attempted the crossing 22 times!

Wolffe had lived in London for a few years and trained at Brighton for his attempts. On several occasions, he had near misses. Three times he got to within a mile of the opposite coast and once, in 1911, he failed by yards.

Like many swimmers, Wolffe was accompanied by pace-makers, including his trainers. On one occasion, a Pipe-Major Nicholls played his bagpipes on the following boat, adjusting his rhythm to match the swimmer's rate of 29 to 32 strokes per minute. At other times, a gramophone record was played for the same purpose.

For all this help, however, and his undoubted efforts, Jabez Wolffe never managed to put his name on the list of successful Channel swimmers.

The first Scot to do so was W.E. Barnie from Portobello. Born in 1896, 'Ned' Barnie became a teacher of science and won the Military Medal in the First World War. Scottish Amateur 880-yards freestyle champion in 1924 and 1925, he was also president of the Scottish Amateur Swimming Association in 1946.

Barnie first swam the Channel in the *Daily Express* Cross-Channel Race on 22 August 1950, when he finished fifth of the nine finishers (thirteen failed to finish) in the France–England crossing.

A year later, with the race in the opposite direction, he repeated the feat, becoming the first man to swim it both ways, and also the oldest man ever to do it, a distinction he held for 28 years.

Barnie was a dedicated swimmer who swam in the Forth every day, sometimes having to break the ice on the water. For his seventieth birthday treat, he swam from Fisherrow, Musselburgh, to Portobello, a distance of two miles. Ned Barnie continued swimming right up until his death on Christmas Day, 1983.

Was she denied a deserved win? Elenor Gordon

In 1950, 16-year-old Elenor Gordon set off with a chaperone for the six-week voyage to the Empire Games in New Zealand. She returned with the first gold medal by a Scotswoman in those games. Her victory in the 200 yards breaststroke also made her the youngest ever Scottish gold medallist.

Two years later, at the Olympic games in Helsinki, she was the only Briton to win a swimming medal. But the final was controversial. It included both breaststroke and butterfly swimmers, the butterfly being a new style and a faster one. Gordon finished third to two butterfly swimmers.

VARIOUS SPORTS

ANGLING

Angling, 1920s–1980s

Scottish waters and Scottish anglers have reached the top ten in a number of different categories of angling.

The largest ever species of fresh-water fish ever caught in Great Britain was a salmon by Miss G.W. Ballantyne on the River Tay in Scotland in 1922, and it weighted 64 lb. The heaviest ever trout caught was on Loch Lomond by Tommy Morgan in 1945, and it weighed in at 47 lb.

The largest sea-trout ever caught in Great Britain was by Samuel Burgoyne on the River Leven in Scotland in 1989 and it weighed 22 lb 8oz. And in the various species of salt-water fish caught around Great Britain, the largest ever caught was a common skate, by R. Banks of Tobermory in Mull in 1986, and that weighed in at 227 lb.

BALL GAMES

Carterhaugh ba' game

An early example of what passed for competitive sport in Scotland took place at Carterhaugh, the flat open plain at the confluence of the Rivers Ettrick and Yarrow, on 4 December 1815.

Organised by Sir Walter Scott, this was a match between the houses of Home and Buccleuch. Scott wrote some verses to anticipate the event and after some prompting, he also received a few words from James Hogg, the Ettrick Shepherd.

From the Buccleuch side came the Soutars of Selkirk, led by their chief magistrate Dr Clarkson and wearing sprigs of fir in their bonnets; while the Shepherds of Yarrow, led by the Earl of Home with James

Hogg as his deputy, were distinguished by similarly placed sprigs of heather.

The contest was played with many hundreds on each side and was essentially a game between townsfolk and countrymen. Scott always referred to it as a 'football' match but both participants and spectators objected, stating that it was in fact, a game of 'handball'.

The 'balls' were made from leather with wool inside. The 'goals' were set a mile apart and the Duke of Buccleuch started the first game by throwing the ball in the air. Immediately, the two sides – with possibly as many as 750 men taking part – rushed together to reach it, and the pushing, shoving and sweating began. For a long time, a stalemate ensued, but then the 'townies' managed to score and a break was taken for refreshments.

After some arguments over defections from teams, the second game began, won some three hours later by the Shepherds. Sir Walter Scott and the Duke of Buccleuch immediately set in hand pereparations for a third game, but arguments sprang up again among the tired throng and there was no further play.

The Kirkwall ba' game

Every Christmas and New Year's Day, the shopkeepers and householders of Kirkwall board up their doors and windows in preparation for the traditional ba' game.

The exact origins of the game are unclear but they are thought to date from some early Yuletide celebrations. It has been played in Orkney since the middle of the 17th century and the style of the contest has changed over the years. Originally, the ba' was kicked and rarely handled, whereas today it is picked up and carried.

For many years the New Year Ba' was the more important but in the late 19th century the Christmas Ba' increased in popularity and nowadays both are important occasions.

The ba' game is a form of street rugby which starts at Mercat Cross in front of the cathedral. At exactly one o'clock, the ba' is thrown up into the huge crowd gathered there and the two teams – the Uppies, born south of the cathedral, and the Doonies, those born to the north side – begin their battle.

The aim is to get the ball into one of the goals. In the case of the Uppies, their target is a wall in the south of the town; while the Doonies try to put the ball into the harbour at the north. As you can imagine, tactics are fairly basic, with a huge scrum usually developing round the player holding the ball and each side trying to move towards the opposition goal.

There are no particular rules in the ba' game but even though there is a fair bit of rough-and-tumble, there would appear to be still an air of courtesy among the players. Quick breaks are seldom evident due to the number of players involved, but there have been occasions when the ba' was sneaked through houses or across rooftops in a bid to score.

For every game a new ba' is specially made of leather with a cork-dust filling, and when one team manages to reach the opposition goal, the ba' is presented to a player from the winning side to take home.

CHESS

Blindfolded: George Koltanowski, 1937

Chess Grandmaster George Koltanowski took on 34 opponents in Edinburgh on 20 September 1937 in a simultaneous display. Just to make matters more complicated for him, he wore a blindfold throughout the exhibition, which lasted for 13.5 hours. Of the 34 matches, Koltanowski won 24 and drew 10.

CROQUET

Anyone for croquet? David Johnstone Macfie

David Johnstone Macfie was born in 1828 and lived at Borthwick Hall, Midlothian. He was Scottish croquet champion from 1870–75 and again in 1879; he is also believed to have introduced the game to Scotland. The Scottish Championship was usually held at Moffat and was in advance of English ideas in that the event was open to both men and women. Indeed, in 1876 and 1877 Macfie lost his title to Miss Jessie Forrest.

CURLING

The Grand Match

The most spectacular curling match in Scotland – when it comes off – is the 'Grand Match' between the North and South of Scotland on outside ice.

The 'Nation's Bonspiel' is a magnificent sight, with six hundred rinks of curlers fighting it out on one of Scotland's lochs. However, 7 inches (135 mms) of good black ice are needed for the match and too often all the planning for the event is in vain.

The first Grand Match was held at Penicuik on 15 January 1847, with 96 curlers taking part; the second, on Linlithgow Loch in 1848, attracted 280.

In 1851, at a meeting of the Royal Club, it was proposed that they should have 'a piece of ground which could be flooded for the purpose of affording a safe sheet of ice for the Grand Matches'. Mrs Home Drummond Stirling Moray of Abercairney granted permission to use her land at Carsebeck for the purpose, at a rental of £15 for 63 acres from November to February each season.

By flooding this area, 25 matches were played between 1853 and 1935. The last match there, on 24 December 1935 (on 5 inches of ice, the safety minimum at that time) attracted 2,576 competitors, whose final hour on the ice was rather spoiled by a sudden thaw. Curlers suddenly found themselves up to their calves in water!

Since that first event in 1847, 38 Grand Matches in total have been held, of which 33 were on outside ice, 1 in November, 9 in December, 16 in January and 7 in February. The other 5 matches were held indoors in the Edinburgh and Glasgow Ice Rinks, although these were not pleasing to the traditionalists. They believe a Grand Match in an indoor ice rink is a contradiction in terms.

There have been three Grand Matches since the Second World War. These were held at Loch Leven in 1959 and the Lake of Menteith in both 1963 and 1979. Since then, in spite of much enthusiasm every year, there has not been enough of a cold snap to enable the event to go ahead. And with global warming apparently increasing, could we have seen the last outdoor Grand Match?

Scots roar their way to the gold

On an exciting evening in February 2002 in Salt Lake City, Utah, USA, Great Britain's women curlers won the country's first Winter Olympics gold medal for 18 years. The all-Scots quintet of Rhona Martin, Fiona MacDonald, Margaret Morton, Janice Rankin and Debbie Knox clinched the title with the last stone of the final end.

With Great Britain and Switzerland locked on 3–3, Rhona Martin showed nerves of steel as she played her last stone. A capacity attendance in the stadium and a huge world-wide audience watched in admiration as her stone nudged the Swiss counter out of the circle before nestling near the middle. It was Great Britain's first Winter Games gold medal since Jane Torvill and Christopher Dean in 1984.

CYCLING

Robert Millar

Robert Millar became the first Briton to win the King of the Mountains title in the Tour de France, an award he picked up in 1984. His fourth place in that tour is also the best result by any Briton.

Millar was born in Glasgow in 1958 and showed a precocious talent for the sport, becoming British Amateur Champion in 1978, at the age of 19. He then moved to the ACBB club in Paris, which had produced the likes of Stephen Roche and Shay Elliott.

Quickly showing that he intended to match their form, Millar won his first race with ACBB, then added another 12 wins to become the best amateur in France. In 1979 he again won the British title and finished fourth in the world's amateur championship after wrenching his foot loose in the final sprint. That near-miss got him a contract with Peugeot.

The following three years were ones of disappointment. Millar did not get on with Peugeot's manager, Maurice de Meur, and did not ride the Tour de France till Roland Berland took over in 1983. In that year's tour, Millar broke away on one stage, winning by 6 seconds and moving up 56 places to 27.

That also helped his position in the mountains competition, in which he eventually finished second, although on stage 13 he became the first Briton to wear the polka-dot jersey, allocated to the leader in the mountains race.

A year later, Millar won the mountains title outright and finished fourth overall, behind Laurent Fignon, Bernard Hinault and Greg Lemond.

The flying Scot: Graeme Obree

The sport of cycling does not often get a mention in the mainstream British media, which tends to concentrate on cricket, football and occasionally tennis in the week of Wimbledon. The Tour de France might get a mention but you have to search for it in the depth of the papers.

In 1993, however, only for a very brief period and perhaps for all the wrong reasons, that was all to change courtesy of one man, Graeme Obree, when he smashed the World One Hour Record.

At that time not many cyclists or enthusiasts outwith the Scottish Club scene would have known who Graeme was. So it was a little surprising when he not only beat the Hour Record but he achieved it on a machine that he had built himself, and one which included bearings that he'd managed to rescue from an old washing machine, a point the media did not fail to notice.

What the press did not seem to recognise was Obree's real athletic ability and his determination to beat a world record previously only attempted by the top European professionals at the height of their careers and using the best technology.

Obree's first attempt at the World Hour Record took place at the Olympic track in Hamar, Norway. The previous day he had been unable to get near the record distance. However, on the Saturday, the day on which he was due to leave, he felt so good and was so convinced that he could achieve a new record that he managed to persuade officials to let him try again. He broke Francesco Moser's record by 445 metres, covering 51.596 kilometres.

Despite what the public thought, his bicycle (which he later coined 'Old Faithful') wasn't built from a washing-machine. However, he did hand build it and it did incorporate a piece of metal tubing that he found when he was out on a training ride, parts from a BMX and also a bearing taken from a washing machine.

What was unusual was Obree's position on the bike. The arrangement of the handlebars allowed him to get stretched out, but also to adopt a position with his arms tucked in out of the way. This wasn't fancied by other riders looking to attempt the record, but it was soon adopted in various forms by them all, including the great Francesco Moser, once the potential was realised. At the World Track Championships in the same year, Obree went on to take the 4,000-metres Pursuit Championship, again in a record time, firmly establishing himself a strong amateur up there with the fastest and the best.

Obree's Hour Record only stood for six days as Chris Boardman exceeded the distance by a further 674 metres (52.270 kilometres). Not content with second place though, Obree came back the following year, in April 1994, and at Bordeaux beat the record again at 52.713 kilometres. Unfortunately, the following month the UCI changed the rules in an attempt to outlaw the position, and when Obree turned up at the World Championships and got through the initial rounds the officials decided to employ the new rules and disqualify him.

Obree refused to be beaten and in 1995 he turned up with a more conventional framed machine plus a modified position that put his arms out Superman style. He won the 4,000-metres World Track Championship in record time. Unfortunately, it was to no avail, and in 1996, with everyone using the Superman position to great effect, the UCI again rewrote the rules regulating the forward position of the handlebars, and used those same rules 'to prevent technical advantage'.

Obree's domestic achievements included winning the RTTC title for 50 miles in 1 hour 39 minutes 1 second; and the 10 miles at 18 minutes 27 seconds, which stood from 1993 to 1996. He also won the RTTC 25 Miles in 48 minutes 55 seconds. On the track he won the British 4,000-metres Pursuit from 1993 to 1996; and in Scotland, on the road, was the national 10-Mile Timed Trial Champion between 1988 and 1992.

DARTS

Darts championships

The World Professional Darts Championship is the highlight of the sport and has been running since 1978. The first Scot to win the event was Jocky Wilson in 1982.

Born in Kirkcaldy, Wilson worked as a miner in Seafield Colliery. However, while unemployed in 1979, he won the Butlin's Grand Masters tournament, collecting a prize of £500. Within a year, Wilson had reached the world's top eight in the professional rankings.

In 1982, at the Jollees nightclub, Stoke, Wilson beat John Lowe of England to win the Embassy World Professional Championship Trophy, the first Scot to do so. After a few poor seasons he repeated the feat in 1989, beating England's Eric Bristow at the Lakeside Country Club, Surrey.

In 1997, at that latter venue, Les Wallace became the second Scot to take the title when he beat Marshall James of Wales. Wallace was also the first left-hander to win the event and he was certainly the first to wear a kilt in doing so!

In the women's championship, which began in 2001, no Scot has yet won the top prize, although Anne Kirk finished runner-up to Trina Gulliver of England in 2003.

DOG RACING

Greyhound Derby, 1928

Since its inception in 1927 only one dog from Scotland has ever won the Greyhound Derby.

For the second year of the competition, the entire event was held at the White City in London and had attracted a total field of 91. Of these, fifty-six were from London tracks, ten from Manchester, six Birmingham-based, four Edinburgh, three Dublin, two Belfast and two Bristol, as well as single entries from Glasgow, Liverpool, Portsmouth, Nottingham, Cardiff, Bradford, Brighton and Slough.

The entrant from Edinburgh, Boher Ash, was purchased in a rather unusual way. The Greyhound Racing Authority sent a draft of dogs up to the capital, where they performed in races at Powderhall to show their form. A local enthusiast, Mrs Stokes, took a fancy to one of them, bought it for £25 and sent it to Tom Johnston at the Powderhall track for training.

In the first two rounds of the 1928 competition, Boher Ash looked good. In the semi-final, however, he was very slow out of the trap and just managed third – good enough to reach the final but a disappointing performance all the same.

Five of the finalists were London-based, with Boher Ash the only visitor. Four of the six runners were owned by women. Security was intense on the night, with a special detective on duty in the kennels.

Favourite for the title was Fabulous Figure, at 11–10, owned by the coursing fanatic Mrs Ruth Fawcett. From the off, though, Boher Ash, at 5-1 fourth favourite, took advantage of his trap one draw to make an excellent start. By halfway, he had slipped back to second but in the final push he came through to win by half-a-length from Fabulous Figure, with Musical Box a further neck away in third.

The night turned out to be a good one for Mrs Stokes, in several ways. Firstly, she became the owner of the first Scottish winner of the Greyhound Derby; secondly, for a dog costing only £25, she picked up the sum of £1,500, the biggest winner's cheque from the first race in 1927 till the start of the Second World War; and thirdly, she had backed Boher Ash, whose winning price of 5-1 was the second-best in those years.

HORSE RACING

The Scottish Grand National, 1920–94

The Scottish Grand National began life as the West of Scotland Grand National at Bogside (North of Ayr) in May 1867 over three miles.

In 1881 the name was changed to The Scottish Grand National and the distance increased to 3 miles 7 furlongs. Between the two World Wars, three horses won the Grand National at Aintree and the 'Scottish' version; Music Hall (1920 Scottish, 1922 Grand National), Sergeant Murphy (1922, Grand National 1923) and Kellsboro Jack (1935, Grand National 1933). On either side of the Second World War, two horses stamped their name on the event. Southern Hero became the first horse to win the event thee times (1934, 1936, 1939) the latter at the age of 14; and that feat was emulated by Queen's Taste (1953, 1954 and 1956).

Bogside closed in 1965 and the race was transferred to Ayr, where it has become one of the great spectacles of the jumping season. Red Rum won in 1974 only a few weeks after his second win at Aintree and 'Rummy' remains the only horse to have won both races in the same year.

Other horses to win the Grand National and its Scottish equivalent are Little Polvier (Ayr 1987, Aintree 1989) and Earth Summit (Ayr 1994, Aintree 1998).

The Grand National – The only Scots-trained winner

Bred by Mrs R. Digby, the 10-year-old Rubstic became the first Scottish-trained winner of the Grand National in 1979, its first attempt at the event. Owned by Mr John Douglas, trained by John Leadbetter at

Denholm and ridden by Maurice Baines, Rubstic won by one-and-a-half lengths from Zongalero, at a good price of 25–1. Highland Wedding, winner ten years before in 1969, although bred by John Caldwell at Prestwick, was trained by Toby Balding in England.

Willie Carson – the star jockey from Stirling

Willie Carson rode his first race at Redcar in 1959 but had to wait until July 1962 for his first win, which came at Catterick. In the following 34 years, Carson rode a total of 3,282 winners, notching 100 for a season on 23 occasions. He also had 17 Classic successes, 4 in each of the Derby, the Oaks and the 2000 Guineas; 2 in the 1000 Guineas; and 3 in the St Leger. Willie Carson's total of wins puts him into fourth place in the all-time list, behind Sir Gordon Richards, Lester Piggott and Pat Eddery.

ICE HOCKEY

On thick ice: ice hockey in Scotland, c 1140–1982

The origins of ice hockey go back a long way:

1140s:	People were skating by that date. There were reports of Vikings tying animal bone to the underside of their boots to make primitive ice skates.
1682:	Edinburgh Skating Club is formed – Britain's oldest skating organisation.
1908:	First ice-hockey game played in Scotland, at Crossmyloof in Glasgow.
1913:	British Ice Hockey Association is founded.
1929:	Scottish Ice Hockey Association formed.
1954:	First British League formed. Five senior clubs for England, seven from Scotland.
1955:	Only seven teams enter the second season of the British League, with Paisley Pirates the only Scottish side.

1959:   Paisley: now the Mohawks – win the British title.

1960–1970s: Serious ice hockey mainly in Scotland and the north of England. The 'ICY' Smith Cup is the forerunner of the British Championship and Murrayfield Racers win it eight times between 1965 and 1980. Other Scots winners are Fife Flyers, Ayr Bruins and Glasgow Dynamos.

1981–82:   Both the English and Scottish National leagues are revived, 25 years after the old Scottish and English leagues were held. The top four teams – Streatham Redskins and Blackpool Seagulls from England, Murrayfiield Racers and Dundee Rockets from Scotland – meet at Streatham to decide the British Championship, with Dundee beating Streatham 3–2 in the final.

An ice–hockey first: Tony Hand, 1970s

Starting his career in senior hockey at the age of 13 with Murrayfield Racers, Tony Hand became the first British player to score 1,000 goals.

In 1986 he also became the first British-trained player to be drafted into the North American National Hockey League, taken up by the Edmonton Oilers.

JUDO

George Kerr

Born in 1937, George Kerr is one of only two people in the UK to hold a 9th Dan in Judo (the highest Dan, the tenth, is held by very few, most of whom are in Japan). Kerr won a gold medal at the 1957 European Championships and was British Open champion in 1966 and 1968. He also coached a double Olympic champion, the Austrian Peter Seisenbacher.

ROWING

William Duthie Kinnear: Gold rowing, 1912

William Duthie Kinnear was the third Scot to win an individual Olympic event, after Launceston Elliott and Wyndham Halswelle.

Wally Kinnear was born in 1880 at Laurencekirk. By the beginning of the 20th century he was working in the drapery trade in his own town but the bright lights beckoned and he moved to London in 1902. At the Debenham company, colleagues introduced him to rowing, and within a short time, Kinnear was hooked on it.

He joined the Cavendish Rowing Club, quickly making a name for himself at sculling before joining the more prestigious Kensington Rowing Club in 1905. During the following five years, he won numerous events along the Thames, becoming one of the world's leading scullers by taking two major titles, the Diamonds at Henley and the Wingfield, in both 1910 and 1911.

In 1912, Kinnear was chosen for the Great Britain team at the Stockholm Olympics, where he comfortably won his heat and semi-final. In the final, he faced formidable opposition in Vierman of Belgium and Butler of Canada, but Kinnear proved up to the task, winning easily by nine seconds to retain the trophy for Britain, Harry Blackstaffe having won in 1908.

Two years later, Kinnear was in the Royal Air Force, with which he served for the duration of the First World War. Afterwards, his interest in rowing was mainly confined to coaching and administration but Wally Kinnear enjoyed a along and varied career before his death in London in 1974.

SHINTY

Shinty

The game of shinty can be traced back to the earliest days of Scotland's heritage. Its demands of skill, speed, stamina and courage made it a perfect exercise for a warrior people. Through the years, the game was played according to a plethora of unwritten rules and local variations. However, like many other team sports, shinty became more organised in the latter half on the 19th century.

Important moments in Shinty

1861:   Aberdeen University Shinty Club becomes the first constituted club in the sport.

1870:   Edinburgh Camanachd Club claims to be the first 'independent' club.

1870s: The first history, written rules and elementary coaching manual is brought out.

1877:   The Glasgow Celtic Society, originally formed in 1856, circulates a set of rules to every shinty club in the south of Scotland.

1879:   The Glasgow Celtic Society hosts the first major competition in shinty. In the inaugural final, Glasgow Cowal beat Renton 6–0.

1880:   The Strathglass Camanachd Club wass formed and brought out an up-to-date set of rules.

1887–88: Glen Urquhart met Strathglass in two strongly contested matches in Inverness. These kindled enthusiasm for the game in the north.

1889:   Badenoch played Lochaber in an epic contest at Laggan which showed the superiority of the leather ball.

1893:   Kingussie and Glasgow Cowal met in a historic match which demonstrated the need for standardised rules.

1893:   The Canamachd Association was formally instituted on 10 October in the Victoria Hall, Kingussie. Initial draft rules agreed upon suggested 16 players-a-side, with pitch of 200 yards long and 150 broad.

1894:   The Camanachd Association held its first AGM. The rules were revised to permit teams of 12 players, and a pitch of 150 yards long by 70 broad.

1896:   The 'Scottish Cup' or more correctly, the 'Camanachd Association Challenge Cup' was inaugurated. The cup was purchased by the association with public donations and nowadays is contested by the eight teams in the Premier League and the last eight in the Balliemore Cup competition.

Winners

Kingussie 21, Inveraray 3, Beauly 3, Oban 2, Ballachullish 4, Caberfeidh 2, Kyles Athletic 20, Oban Celtic 5, Newtonmore 28, Inverness 1, Furnace 1, Lovat 1, Kilmallie 1, Glasgow Mid-Argyll 1, Skye 1, Fort William 1, Oban Camanachd 1.

1923:   The Sutherland Cup is introduced, a national competition to encourage junior teams.

1937:   The Schools Camanachd Association is formed.

1974:   The first in-depth debate on shinty is held.

1980:   After 20 hours of discussion, the Future of Shinty Committee agrees a new Camanachd Association structure embracing all individual bodies.

TABLE TENNIS

Scotswoman with a bat: Helen Elliot Hamilton

Born in 1927, Helen Elliot Hamilton twice won the Ladies' World Doubles Table Tennis Championship, each time with a different non-Scots partner.

In 1949, she and her Hungarian partner Gizi Fakas lived up to their reputations as strong favourites: one year later, though, Hamilton and her new partner, Englishwoman Dora Beregi, won against the odds.

In a long career, Hamilton won International Open Singles titles in Ireland, Wales, Germany and Belgium; International Doubles titles in Scotland, Ireland, Wales, England, Holland, Belgium and Germany; and was National Open Singles Champion of Scotland on thirteen occasions.

TENNIS

Was he the first Scottish Wimbledon champion? Donald Budge

Donald Budge, a tough competitor from California, had the distiction of becoming the first player to win all four Grand Slam titles in the same year. He was also the first man to win the triple crown at Wimbledon and he did that two years running..

Budge's topspin backhand drive was a formidable weapon, especially on a return of service, but in truth his whole game was sound. In the 1937 Wimbledon final, he scored an emphatic straight-set win over the German, Gottfried von Cramm, although at Forest Hills a few weeks later in the US championship, Budge needed five sets to overcome the same opponent.

Budge's four victims in the Grand Slam finals of 1938 all came from different countries – John Bromwich in Australia, Roderick Menzel of Czechoslovakia in France, Britain's 'Bunny' Austin at Wimbledon and fellow American Gene Mako at Forest Hills. He won the 1937 and 1938 Wimbledon men's doubles titles with Mako and the mixed with Alice Marble.

A fine record. But you may be wondering why his name should appear in this book? Well, Donald Budge's father had played a few matches for Rangers' reserve team before emigrating to the USA. By modern rules, that would make him a Scot and therefore the first Scot to win the Grand Slam in tennis!

WALKING

The walking captain: Captain Robert Barclay Allardice

Before the advent of team sports, walking and running were major participant activities. One of the stars of the time was Captain Robert Barclay Allardice, a man renowned for his remarkable walking feats.

'Captain Barclay', as he was commonly called, walked 90 miles in just over 20 hours in 1801 for a fee of 5,000 guineas. In 1809, he went even further and walked a mile every 1,000 hours. Twice a week, he would walk the 51 miles from his home to Turriff, take his pack of hounds across another 20 miles of country, and then walk the 51 miles back home again.

Captain Barclay was also a noted boxing trainer, one of whose pupils, Tom Cribb, became bare-knuckle champion of the world in 1808.

GENERAL

A fine all-rounder: Leslie Balfour-Melville

Leslie Balfour-Melville was one of the great sporting all-rounders of his time, whose Scotland career – as an opening bat and wicketkeeper – lasted for 40 years!

Born in 1854, 'L.M.' was a schoolboy at Edinburgh Academy when he made the top score for an Edinburgh XXII against George Parr's England XI; later, while playing for – and captaining – the Gentlemen of Scotland, his knock of 73 contributed to their 47-run defeat of the visiting Australians at Raeburn Place on 27–28 July 1882.

Before then, his fine form on the rugby field for Edinburgh Accies had gained him an international appearance. In the second match Scotland ever played against England at Kennington Oval, on 5 February 1872, in the 20-a-side team, 'L.M.' was among the backs as Scotland lost by one drop-goal to one goal, one drop-goal and two tries.

Melville Balfour had a very varied and successful sporting career. He played for the MCC; was Scottish Lawn Tennis Champion in 1879; won the Scottish long-jump title; won the British Amateur Golf Championship in 1895; became captain of the Royal and Ancient Golf Club in 1906; was elected president of both the Scottish Cricket and Rugby Unions; and in his sixtieth year (1913), made three centuries!

BBC Sports Personality of the Year: Ian Black

Since this award was first presented to the athlete Chris Chataway in 1954, there have been only three Scots winners. The stories of both Jackie Stewart (1973) and Liz McColgan (1991) are discussed elsewhere in this book but in any case, they had to take second and third place in the Scottish list. The first was an Aberdonian who picked up the award in 1958.

Ian Black was a swimmer, which in the late '50s and early '60s, in the days of black-and-white TV, was a very popular sport.

In 1958 Black won three gold medals in the European Championships at 400 and 1500 metres freestyle, and 200 metres butterfly, along with a 220 yard butterfly gold and silvers at 440 yards freestyle and 4 x 220 yards relay at the British Empire Games.

His one world record came in the 440 yard individual medley; he took fourth places at 400 metres and the 4 x 200 metres relay event in the Rome Olympics of 1960. Black actually dead-heated with Australia's Jon Konrads for bronze in the 400 metres but was relegated to fourth on a technicality. Black then retired, although he came back to the sport for a short time in 1962 when he set a new European record for the 200 metres freestyle. During his career, he had also set European records at 800 and 1500 metres freestyle, 200 metres butterfly and 400 metres individual medley.

Robert Burns and sport

At the time of Robert Burns, in the late 18th century, organised sport was probably limited to archery, coursing, hunting and the occasional 'ball-game' on special occasions in different areas of the country.

However, curling was obviously being played and as we can see in these words from *Tam Samson's Elegy*, Burns seems to have had some knowledge of its ploys:

When Winter muffles up his cloak,
And binds the mire like a rock,
When to the loughs the curlers flock
    Wi'gleesome speid,
Wha will they station at the 'cock' ?
    Tam Samson's dead!

He was the king o' a' the core,
To guard, to draw, or wick a bore,
Or up the rink like Jehu roar,
    In Time o' need;
But now he lags on Deaths 'hog-score' –
    Tam Samson's dead!

Empire Games: review

In the late 1920s it was proposed that one of the cities in the far-flung British Empire should host a gathering where competitors from various countries could compete against each other in a series of sports. These were to be called the British Empire Games. The host cities were: 1930, Hamilton, Ontario, Canada; 1934, London, England; 1938, Sydney, Australia; 1950, Auckland, New Zealand.

For the next four gatherings, the name changed to the British Empire and Commonwealth Games: 1954, Vancouver, British Columbia, Canada; 1958, Cardiff, Wales; 1962, Perth, Australia; 1966, Kingston, Jamaica.

After Kingston, the name changed again, this time to the British Commonwealth Games, and within the following 16 years the capital of Scotland would twice host the event: 1970, Edinburgh, Scotland; 1974, Christchurch, New Zealand; 1978, Edmonton, Alberta, Canada; 1982, Brisbane, Queensland, Australia; 1986, Edinburgh, Scotland.

Since 1990 – and for all future games – the name used is the Commonwealth Games: 1990, Auckland, New Zealand; 1994, Victoria, British Columbia, Canada; 1998, Kuala Lumpur, Malaysia; 2002, Manchester, England; 2006, Melbourne, Australia; 2010, New Delhi, India.

SCOTTISH SPORTS
HALL OF FAME

PART 1, 2002

Please note: Cross references are provided where more infromation is to be found in this book.

During 2002, an initial list of 100 Scottish sporting stars was drawn up by a panel of experts and 50 were selected to form the Scottish Sports Hall of Fame. These are:

Louise Aitken Walker (1960–): The first woman to win outright a national driving championship in Britain. She won the Ladies' World Rally Championship in 1990.

Alister Allan (1944–): Scotland's most successful competitor in the Commonwealth Games. He won three gold, three silver and four bronze at shooting. Allan also collected Olympic silver and bronze medals.

Captain Robert Barclay Allardice (1779–1854) *Walking* p. 235

Tommy Armour (1894–1968) *Golf* p. 141

Leslie Balfour-Melville (1854–1937) *General sports* p. 235

Jim Baxter (1939–2001): A Rangers legend. Collected 34 caps for Scotland.

Ian Black (1941–) Swimming, see *General* p. 236

Sir Chay Blyth (1940–) *Sailing* p. 203

James Braid (1870–1950) *Golf* p. 139

Billy Bremner (1942–1997): 54 caps for Scotland and 73 matches for Leeds United.

Ken Buchanan (1945–) *Boxing* p. 23

Sir Matt Busby (1909–1994): manager of Manchester United when they won the European Cup in 1968.

Willie Carson (1942–) *Horse racing* p. 229

John Cattanach (1885–1915): One of the outstanding shinty players of his generation. Scored eight goals when Newtonmore beat Furnace in the Camanachd Cup final in 1909 – still a record today.

Jim Clark (1936–1968) *Motor sports* p. 158

Kenny Dalglish (1951–) *Football* p. 82

Mike Denness (1940–) *Cricket* p. 45

Donald Dinnie (1837–1916) *Athletics* p. 6

Launceston Elliot (1874–1930) *Gold medallists* p. 129

John Greig (1942–): 44 caps for Scotland and captain of Rangers when they won the European Cup-Winners' Cup in 1972.

Gavin Hastings (1962–): captain of Scotland on 20 occasions and also captain of the British Lions on the New Zealand tour of 1993.

Dougal Haston (1940–1977) *Climbing* p. 38

Sir Peter Heatley (1924–) *Swimming* p. 213

Andy Irvine (1951–): attacking full-back who gained 51 caps for Scotland, 15 of them as captain.

Jimmy Johnstone (1944–): one of the finest wingers Scotland ever produced; a member of the Celtic team which won the European Cup in 1967.

Ellen King (1909–1994): she won six British swimming championships, set two world records and collected two silver medals in the 1928 Olympics.

Denis Law (1940–): the youngest player ever to be capped by Scotland; still holds the scoring record (with Kenny Dalglish) of 30 international goals.

Benny Lynch (1913–1946) *Boxing* p. 24

Walter McGowan (1942–) *Boxing* p. 32

Bobby McGregor (1944–) *Swimming* p. 213

Bob McIntyre (1928–1962) *Motor sports* p. 160

Billy McNeill (1941–): captain of the Lisbon Lions, the first British team to win the European Cup.

G.P.S. McPherson (1903–1981): captain of the first Scotland side to complete rugby's Grand Slam in 1925.

Dick McTaggart (1935–) *Boxing* p. 31

Young Tom Morris (1851–1875) *Golf* p. 139

Mark Coxon Morrison (1878–1945): captained Scotland on the rugby field on 15 of his 23 cap career.

Jackie Paterson (1920–1966) *Boxing* p. 26

Rodney Pattison (1943–) *Sailing* p. 204

Nancy Riach (1927–1947) *Swimming* p. 213

Belle Robertson (1936–) *Golf* p. 143

Bill Shankly (1913–1981): manager of Liverpool when they won three English league titles.

Robert Wilson Shaw (1913–1979): captain of the Scottish team which won the Triple Crown in 1938.

Winnie Shaw (1947–1992): Scotland's most successful woman tennis player, she reached the quarter-finals at Wimbledon in 1970 and 1971; she also reached the semi-finals of the Ladies Doubles in 1972.

Jock Stein (1922–1985): manager of Celtic when they won the European Cup in 1967. In a 13-year career at the helm, he also led the club to ten League Championships, eight Scottish Cups and six League Cups.

Ian Stewart (1949–): winner of the 5,000 metres in the Commonwealth Games in 1970 and the world cross-country title in 1973.

Sir Jackie Stewart (1939–) *Motor sports* p. 157

Alan Wells (1952–) *Athletics* p. 3

David Wilkie (1954–) *Gold medallists* p. 126

Jim Watt (1948–) *Boxing* p. 30

PART 2, 2003

In December 2003, fourteen Scottish sporting legends were inducted into the Scottish Sports Hall of Fame at a presentation in Edinburgh. They were:

Old Tom Morris (1821–1908) *Golf* p. 138
Wyndham Halswelle (1882–1915) *Olympics* p. 164
Jimmie Guthrie (1897–1937) *Motor sports* p. 159
Jessie Valentine (1915–) *Golf* p. 137
Gordon Smith (1925–) *Football* p. 77
Helen Elliot Hamilton (1927–) *Table tennis* p. 233
Elenor Gordon (1933–) *Swimming* p. 215
George Kerr (1937–) *Judo* p. 230
Robert Millar (1958–) *Cycling* p. 223.

The other 5 inductees were:

Bobby Thomson

Born in Glasgow in 1923, Thomson moved to the USA at the age of two. Just after the end of the Second World War he began his baseball career, which ran for 14 years. The highlight came on 3 October 1956, when playing for the New York Giants in a local derby against the Brooklyn Dodgers. The 'Staten Island Scot', as Thomson was known, hit baseball's most famous home run, which gave the Giants a much-needed victory and also the National League pennant. Thomson was voted an All-Star in 1948,1949 and 1952.

Hamish MacInnes

One of the first proponents of modern winter mountaineering, Hamish MacInnes, was equally well known for his efforts on the mountains and his equipment designs. These include the first all-metal ice axe and the

MacInnes mountain-rescue stretchers. He made his first attempt on Everest at the age of 23 in 1953, a low-budget trip with fellow Scot John Cunningham of the Glasgow-based Creagh Dhu Mountaineering Club. Twenty years later, MacInnes was deputy leader of the successful 1975 Everest South-west Face expedition. As well as his many successful climbs, he has written 21 books and is an authority on mountain rescue.

John McNiven

John McNiven had a long and successful weightlifting career, covering 6 Commonwealth Games, 2 bronze medals and 25 Scottish National championship victories. Even after retirement, McNiven continued to excel, organising one of the biggest-ever sports events in Scotland, the World Masters championships, held in Glasgow in 1999. It attracted over 450 competitors. McNiven himself has competed in 18 World Masters events, of which he won 14; and he was first to receive the World Masters Weightlifting Hall of Fame Award in 1993.

George McNeill

A highly talented sprinter, McNeill was unable to compete as an amateur due to a short spell as a professional footballer. Forced on to the pro circuit in athletics, he went on to win two of the most famous races in the world: the Powderhall Sprint in 1970 and Australia's Stawell Gift in 1981. In 1971 he ran 110 metres in 11 seconds (equivalent to 10 seconds for the 100 metres); while in 1972 he defeated Olympic 200-metres champion Tommie Smith in a four-race series and was crowned world professional sprint champion.

Finlay Calder

An open-side flanker who played for Scotland between 1986 and 1991, Calder's finest game was probably the Grand Slam decider between Scotland and England at Murrayfield in 1990. His all-action style and competitive attitude helped drive the team on to a memorable win. Calder won 34 caps for Scotland, 7 as captain. He also captained the British Lions in 1989.

Maggi McEleny: a new kind of sports star

And finally. In the last quarter of the 20th century, a new breed of sports star came to prominence. Originally described as handicapped, these men and women put aside their difficulties to reach the top of their chosen sport. Every one deserves our recognition and respect for their achievements but as an example of what they have to go through, let me tell the story of one such heroine.

Maggi McEleny was born in Greenock in February 1965. At the age of eleven, a netball stand fell on her head while at school and shortly afterwards she started to have seizures. Eventually, epilepsy was diagnosed. The attacks were infrequent and relatively mild, so she coped at primary and secondary school with little trouble. However, when she applied to train as a nurse at Inverclyde Royal Hospital, the authorities there rejected her application due to the epilepsy. Maggi re-applied, to the Royal Alexandra Infirmary in Paisley, and this time she was successful. Six months into her course, Maggi suffered a massive epileptic seizure on her way to work. She was rushed to the Southern General in Glasgow, spent the following month in a coma and was a whole year in hospital altogether.

By the time she was allowed home, Maggi was blind and paralysed from the neck down. Her parents, who had been told that she would never recover from these injuries, took her home and looked after her. But Maggi surprised them. Within a year, her sight returned; gradually, she got back the use of her arms, and slowly but surely she learned to dress and feed herself again. She knew she had to adapt and wanted to be independent.

In March 1990, a coach at Port Glasgow Otters Swimming Club, Peter Stanton, a wheelchair user, suggested that Maggi should go along to his disabled club there. On her first night, her mum and dad went along with her, got her out of the wheelchair, balanced her sitting at the side of the pool with her feet in the water and perched themselves on either side.

Peter Stanton came over, told the parents that they had done their bit and that they could now go away. He then told Maggi to get into